The Missing Peace
Creating a Life after Death

By Ian Donaghy

The Missing Peace
Creating a Life After Death

First published 2017

ID Publications, The White House, White House Mews,
Kexby Avenue, York. YO10 3HF 01904 423321

Printed & bound in Great Britain.

British Library Cataloguing in Publication Data.

A catalogue record for this book is available
from the British Library

Book design & layout by Leisa Sherry

Edited by Helen Binks, Anna Oulton, Julian Coles & Inny Hashim

Most photographs courtesy of Ian Donaghy.
Image of butterfly in final chapter courtesy of Yellow Mustang
Photography - Thank you Marc McGarraghy

Original sketches by Chub Perkins

About the Author

Ian Donaghy was born in 1970 and grew up in Tow Law, County Durham before 'emigrating' to York to get a degree in 1988. His infectious enthusiasm and warm, humorous, empathetic approach have made him a popular motivational conference speaker all over the UK and Europe.

Barbara Pointon MBE described his work as "Highly entertaining and deeply thought-provoking".

During a 20 year career teaching young people with learning difficulties Ian was employed by the Home Office to set up inclusion units in schools for vulnerable students focusing on the individual, celebrating what they can do to raise their aspirations and reduce exclusions.

Often deemed a maverick, Ian took his "focus on the individual" into the world of care in 2010 and quickly used his innovative teaching and learning styles to win Care Trainer of the Year at the British Care Awards.

Ian delivers bespoke learning events for clients as diverse as Yorkshire Ambulance Service, Wellburn Care Homes, Wilf Ward Family Trust, Mind, local authorities, large care providers, the NHS and has recently hosted the CQC's Leadership Conference.

In 2014 Ian's book "Dear Dementia: The Laughter and the Tears" was published by Hawker Publications and in under a year reached 24 countries and was included on the Alzheimer's Society Read Well Books on Prescription List of only 25 books for dementia care. Angela Rippon OBE described it as "An inspirational little book and a work of true love".

As a Dementia campaigner and champion for older people Ian has produced and hosted "A Night to Remember" concerts in York theatres attracting audiences of over 1500 raising awareness and funding dementia projects and St. Leonard's Hospice in the city, raising over £100,000 in the past few years.

In 2015 Ian created Xmas Presence - a large party held on Christmas Day to combat loneliness in the elderly which attracted praise from all over the country as well as winning York Press Community Pride Award and Minster FM Local Hero Award. Xmas Presence was also commended by the CEO of Sainsburys.

Ian's popular twitter feed @trainingcarers highlights the ridiculous, fuels debate and champions those who really care with tips and ideas.

At the UK Dementia Congress one speaker asked "Is he the man who makes you cry?"

"No he's the man who makes you THINK..."

"The Missing Peace has been a true labour of love for me. I hope it helps you realise it's not just you... you are not alone... it's a little book with a big heart. I hope it helps..."

"Clock has stopped... time goes on
I'm trying to figure out what to do
Days and nights become one
Now I'm wearing out the soles of my shoes"

- Coming Down From You by J McGough

Contents

Everybody Hurts

Nobody thought this morning when they put the key in door and turned it in the lock, "Well that'll be the last time I'll see you."

You probably have a holiday booked months from now - such is your confidence bordering on the cocksure. You even assume that you will reach the end of this book! Fingers crossed... here we go...

We all think that, like the Titanic, we will leave Southampton and reach New York without incident as icebergs happen to other people. To be fair, if we did die today, it's not our problem... it would be for the people left behind - the survivors.

I have some bad news for you. I'm neither a qualified doctor nor a nurse but I am pretty certain in this diagnosis: You will not get off this rollercoaster alive.

"Everybody hurts sometime"- Michael Stipe.

I would love to have started this book with "Once upon a time," and ended it with, "And they all lived happily ever after..." but life sadly isn't a fairy tale. Goodbye isn't good. Farewell isn't fair.

I was running a bereavement course one day in Whitby where one of the care staff, aged 49, still had all of the family members who saw her being born. Nobody had died. She had lost nobody and had never been to a funeral in half a century. She is quite an exception. I raised my mug of tea to her rare, charmed life.

Unless, like her, you are very fortunate, you will have lost a friend, grandparent, parent, partner, sibling or child. You may have just lost a goldfish. Very rarely do we escape and if we do it's because us leaving will have left someone else grieving.

daughter's hand gently rub my shoulder from the backseat and she said, "Yes, Dad. I know... but you can sort everything else. We all miss Grandma."

Children often astound me with their innate understanding. They see so much. They know more than we give them credit for and put things in such honest, beautiful ways.

I had the most heart-warming day of laughter with my Dad who just seems to get better with age and so much more valuable. As with all good reads, Dad's chapters are more entertaining the further we venture into the book.

I drove away from Weardale and smiled at just how lucky I was to have such a wise, funny, man as my hero. A man who still had the aluminium key ring on his car keys that I made in 1981 smoothed and polished by thirty-four years in his pocket. It was by far the poorest use of emery paper and a hacksaw known to man but he held it as proudly as a Victoria Cross.

I couldn't help but think of all of my friends for whom Father's Day wasn't a day of celebration but an amplifier of other emotions as they hadn't had to buy the obligatory 'Best Dad in the World' card.

There are seven billion people on this planet and yet you may have bought this book because of just one who is no longer here.

This book came about on Father's Day 2015 when I went to visit my Dad with my two children. I diverted and drove past my Mother's graveyard and felt that shudder - reminding me I have a big piece missing from my life. It was like I'd touched the sides playing Operation with my tweezers - that tingle in my nostrils. It was the shiver: the hurt that appears from nowhere. Trying to hide this upset from my young passengers, I took a sharp intake of breath and sucked my teeth but as in many situations when you are desperately trying to show others nothing is wrong with you, they soon realise... there is something wrong with you. I felt my 12 year old

Social media was split down the middle. Half, "Look at my Dad - he's bigger than yours," and half, "Look at my Dad - we miss him so much." Not only were people hurting but at the same time their best friends seemed to be rubbing their noses in it unintentionally.

I suddenly realised that every day is like this... June 10th could be somebody's birthday, prompting the bringing in of cakes for everyone in the office but if it's your late parents' wedding anniversary or your Nana's birthday you may skip the jollity and éclairs to go for an anti-social passive smoke in the rain to get through the day. We are often unaware of the raw state of others and the invisible baggage they may be hauling that day. Armies of one fighting the toughest battle as monoturions (no, it's not a real word but I figured if 'centurions' is 100 then you'd let me off).

Death is the only thing that is certain in our lives and yet discussing it is deemed to be morose, morbid or weird. Nobody looks at you strangely for buying an umbrella knowing one day it will rain.

Death is the last taboo. It is the biggest of all elephants we hoover around in the room. Often the closest of families will talk about anything else rather than address the biggest challenge they will ever face.

I have written this book for one person: you.

I have avoided psychological theory by ologists and iatrists as, having interviewed many of these professionals after losing their own loved ones, I found that even they sometimes leave their theory on the shelf when the objective becomes subjective in their own hardest times. This is a book about ordinary everyday people like you and me who are sharing stories to help others.

There isn't a courtroom on the planet who would execute the ones we love yet it happens every day to people who have never put a step out of line. Too many of my friends were being heartbroken by illness and time. Many were lost for words so I felt the need to start a

conversation with this little book. It is meant to get people to talk but more importantly to listen. This is not a book about death - it is about life and how to be the friend you would love to have. It is about living today not tomorrow.

The book is slightly voyeuristic in that we are peering through peoples'

curtains but with the aim that we will read through the pages saying "I think exactly the same" or "I do that too," allowing us to learn from the mistakes and triumphs of others.

I hope it will highlight that there are no rights and wrongs - only right for you. There will be no plenaries at the end of each story

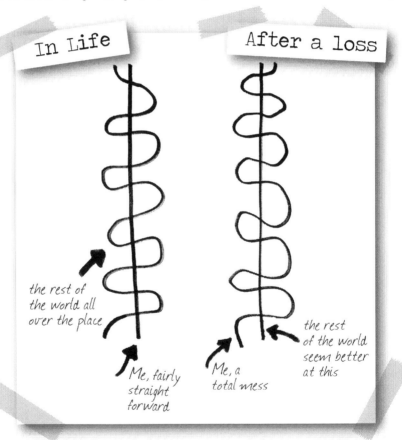

In Life

the rest of the world all over the place

Me, fairly straight forward

After a loss

the rest of the world seem better at this

Me, a total mess

explaining the moral behind it or what you are meant to think like some other books do. YOU read it then YOU decide.

This hasn't been an easy write. It took some tentative approaches to people afraid of how they would react not to being interviewed but to being asked to be interviewed - two years of carrying notebooks, doodling on envelopes, talking into dictaphones in the car, listening to every conversation for pearls of wisdom, sleepless nights, writer's block and limitless procrastination! But it needed to be right and it was too important to be rushed.

The problem is that patience has become extinct. People don't wait any more. Taking your time takes up your time! We need things now in an instant. Even Polaroids disappeared as a minute wait was deemed unimaginable to view the photo you've just taken. "Is there an "App" or a YouTube clip to talk me through step by step?" Some things aren't as easy as changing a fuse or learning the chords to a song you've just heard on the radio. It's going to take you plus time.

This book isn't a magic wand. I would never be so arrogant. It's not a sponge to soak up your hurt or a painkiller to lift off the coffee table to take twice daily. I wish it was as easy as follow this grieving Sat Nav with precise directions without ever hearing "make a U turn". Some may never reach their

destination but I hope this could be a useful gift for a friend when words fail you. I have tried to make it as accessible, thought-provoking, interesting and as engaging a read as possible. It won't kiss it better but it may explain one very important thing. It's not just you. You're not alone.

In life, we often think that we are straightforward and normal but think the rest of the world is all over the place. Yet when someone close to us dies, we suddenly think we are so much worse at coping. We go around thinking that the rest of the world deals with it so much better. This ends up making us feel like islands. While we may be isolated from the mainland, in many cases the same waves crash against our shores. The truth is, we are all broken biscuits - damaged goods, bluffing our way through life hoping nobody notices the hopeless imposters we really are.

"We're never gonna survive unless we get a little crazy" - Seal.

Over two years, I have spoken and interviewed many inspirational people who have lost loved ones. Some commentators hate terms like 'lost loved ones,' considering it euphemistic but I haven't written this for them. Is there anything worse than losing someone you would die for?

This book is a patchwork quilt of conversations, letters, monologues and stories to somehow explain the bespoke survival kits people have created and how they have walked or are still walking through the emotional minefield of grief. We all create some form of survival guide when we need it ourselves but often share it with no-one. In this book, people have been kind enough to open their own tool boxes in order to share what has worked and what has failed. Their footprints may not work for you but some of their ideas might. This book will NOT tell you what to do. It is merely throwing a lot of ideas up in the air - you decide which ones fit you and may help. Grieving isn't a la carte or off the peg. You design it and tailor it to suit all occasions as your

need demands constantly altering it to fit you that day. 'Grieving' may never reach your OUT tray... it's worth remembering that those we may call 'former' alcoholics and drug addicts say they are 'recovering' not 'recovered'.

Will you survive?

Can you thrive?

Any decent gardener can show you how rosebushes can be pruned back to the most barren-looking twigs yet in time they can bloom even better than they did before.

Can you become a better you?

Does that prospect upset you?

I hope these ideas will be shared and provoke debate. The intention is to help people stop feeling alone and instead give a sense of belonging. Give some relief. Give some knowledge that "it's not just me." The idea of the highlighter pen is to read each story and highlight the bits where "I do that". I have also left a blank chapter for you to write down any things that reading these stories will trigger.

In many ways, the book starts from the default setting that you liked and loved the person who has died... but sometimes we don't. Sometimes people aren't missed or loved. They are gone and forgotten. Not everyone was the person we wanted them to be. In some cases the memories may be far better than the person. As Saatchi wrote, "Some lives leave a mark, others a stain." If you can relate to this idea then hopefully this book will have worth for you too as I've tried to explore some of the lesser-seen and lesser-celebrated sides of the grieving process.

Life is just a series of near misses, mishaps, brushes with death, great escapes, all hopefully stitched together with joy. Few of us fear the Reaper but we are terrified of losing those we love. It makes us afraid. We fear if we have something or someone to lose. Perhaps we fear being left behind...

I have spoken to people in homes, pubs, hospitals, care homes and on trains. In every community there are people still standing despite life throwing the most impossible challenges at them from losing siblings, children, parents to having partners murdered. How are these people still putting one foot in the other? What are these survival kits they have created?

If someone close to you dies, you may feel like you can't be more hurt. This is a strange feeling but it can be powerful knowing that you have taken the biggest punch and yet (to your amazement) you're still standing. Like swimming in the sea looking up at a thunderstorm, safe in the knowledge you can't get any wetter.

Life is about what we DO and what we DON'T. So many people live life like they are going to have another one and by the time they realise, it's too late. As very young children we are told that if we are good then good things happen but as we grow up we soon realise that, once again, like the tooth fairy and a big man with a beard and reindeer, grown ups have lied. Bad things do happen to good people. That's not fair.

In job interviews they'd ask "What do you want to be in three years time?"

I'd always answer "Happy" and it always met with a dismissive look down at their clipboard but I still believe I was right. It's what we all want - to be happy with what we have, even if it is less than what you had.

We come into this world to a fanfare yet can leave with a whimper. Some say, "You're born. You hurt. You die. Anything else is a bonus..." Let's hope we look with a little more optimism.

Truth is, very few of us like surprises. We like to know when the bus is coming, what's for tea and what's on next. Even when getting gifts, if we don't like the surprise we ask, "Have you got the receipt?" Understandably, many of us hate uncertainty or anything beyond our control. Guitarist Wilco Johnson spoke of the feeling of elation when he was told he was dying as he knew and it wasn't going to take him by surprise. Life is brutal. We don't truly know when anyone will die or how.

If your birth certificate came with an expiry date in a manila envelope would you open it?

What would you do? What would your priorities be? Financial? Tell people you love them? Go 'round and tell everyone you have bitten your lip in front of what you really think of them? Make sure all 'i's are dotted and 't's are crossed? Getting your affairs in order?"

One honest interviewee laughed, "I'd get into shedloads of debt." Nobody would drive sensible cars.

The good news is that no matter how bad you feel today, if you are reading this you have a 100% survival rate. Congratulations!

I hope you find these stories inspiring, moving and useful. It has been an honour and a pleasure to spend time with such amazing people who are finding their missing peace. You may find you've had it tougher than some and easier than others - we're not deciding who has the blackest cat here - every person's story is individual and how we deal with what life throws at us. We find our own ways, no matter how strange.

We gain so much from shared experience. This book was really written to get my Dad talking. Even if it doesn't sell a single copy, it has already exceeded all expectations as it has broken down barriers, got people thinking, talking and most importantly listening to one another. I hope it does the same for you. Please realise by the end of this that "it's not just you!" and talk now instead of later.

Pick up your highlighter and dab away.

Warning: there may be points in the book where some household dust may get in your eye. I noticed this writing it too so it's definitely not just you...

Save The Last
Dance For Me

I am unsure if the last five years have flown or dragged, but somehow they've passed - and I'm still here.

My masterplan was in place; I'd always worked hard, but now it was time to play. We'd gone on holiday with friends, to Bournemouth, and wandered off one day for a walk together. I remember thinking how lucky we were. We always thought that.

Three months after clearing my desk, the "Happy Retirement" cards were recycled and we were back on yet another dance floor - the perfect end to my first holiday as a free woman. Fun, laughter, good company, music and dancing had been lifelong companions for Steve and me. "Why put off until tomorrow what you can do today?" could easily have been the motto on our coat of arms. Everyone around us was singing "Are we human or are we dancer?" as Steve collapsed.

I fell to the floor beside him as the song continued: "and I'm on my knees, looking for the answer..."

The ambulance arrived, but I knew it was too late. He had always lived life to the full, and had died doing just that. It was the "perfect" death he would have chosen - but not at fifty nine.

Steve and music had always gone hand in hand. We'd immersed ourselves in it, so, for the first year after he died, I cut myself off from all music. I did things I had never done before, like turning the radio off. Every song seemed to tell a story... our story. Even happy songs hurt. In thirty eight years together, inevitably, lots of them had memories for us.

For the first time, I came back to the house and found myself alone - no parents, daughter flown the nest and no husband. My home was empty; I was empty. Music distracted, so I sat in silence. Sunday nights and Bank Holidays hurt most. They seemed the loneliest times of all. I missed the nights out, and then I missed looking back over them, dissecting the gossip.

I was angry as hell. Angry at life and at him. He had got away, scot free. I was left alone with only my friends, Brandy and Lemonade, for company.

I began to spend too much time with these two. I drank to get to sleep, often waking up still on the sofa. I drank to forget, to escape the unthinkable nightmare that had really happened.

One night, I remember being so angry that I hurled a glass of brandy at the wall. I sat on the floor in tears, watching the broken glass and spirit bleed down the wallpaper in slow motion. It didn't give me the release I'd hoped for as all I could think was "Bloody hell! I'll have that to clear up in the morning!"

I never did it again.

That first New Year's Eve, I stayed in and drank two enormous bottles of wine. I never did that again either!

I couldn't face shopping in York, so I travelled twenty miles to Harrogate, hoping to avoid familiar faces. That worked - until one day I saw a couple hand in hand. Their happiness that I once enjoyed hurt me so much that I abandoned my shopping trolley, ran back to the car and broke down in tears. I dreaded having to talk to people, recounting the worst day of my life.

Some people believe that those we've lost walk alongside us and are there when we need them. I'm undecided.

For some reason, I swapped chairs. I moved to sit in what had always been "Steve's armchair". I'd still fall asleep downstairs. One night, I felt a hand wake me up. I wasn't scared. I didn't imagine it. I don't do that kind of thing. It happened and it helped.

I remember giving Steve's clothes away, to the Air Ambulance. I hope he didn't feel

I was throwing him away. I hated signing just my name in birthday cards. That was yet another thing that hurt. On Steve's birthday, I wrote in my diary "Happy birthday! You never wanted to be old. You got your wish!"

In those first years, I didn't dream about Steve once. Perhaps it was too painful, even to dream, then wake up with all bubbles burst.

I swung from angry to fragile, then sad, then thankful, then angry again... how could he have left me? He loved me! I had days when I felt I was winning, climbing the hill, only to slip and fall further down the next day. There was no obvious progression, pattern or improvement. I thought it would never get better - then a social group saved my life. They saved me from loneliness; they saved me from myself.

Not a lonely hearts group, or a dating set up; this was a group to simply combat loneliness with company. The thinking was that if you met up and talked with others who were lonely, friendships could flourish and loneliness might become a thing of the past.

At "FNT" - Fifties 'n' Thereabouts - there was an amazing variety of activities every day! Why these groups aren't everywhere, I don't know. Most of the people were lovely, others less so, but I soon whittled through the chaff to enjoy the nice ones. No-one felt like the odd one out, because we all were!

If I could go back and give myself some good advice, I don't think I would say anything other than: "do whatever you need to do to survive... and go line dancing even if you're no good at it!" Looking back at my diary, I did a hell of a lot of line-dancing - and coffee drinking!

Every day, I asked Steve to keep me safe, to be my strength, to stay near to me. I'd always make the effort to get out of bed and sort my hair. Sometimes, I'd try to avoid the world, but it kept turning up at my door - unwelcome guests, who were actually very brave! I'm so thankful for them now, but at the time I thought "will you just bugger off!"

Writing my diary helped. Writing volumes spoke volumes - a one-way conversation where I played both parts. Asking questions I hoped to answer in character. Initially, I wrote daily, then twice a week, then weekly, then on significant days. Then I just stopped. No reason. No conscious decision. I just stopped clinging to it. Perhaps it was time to let go and venture out onto the ice?

I wasn't the strong woman I had been at work. I was coaxed into seeing a grief counsellor eighteen months after losing Steve, because a friend was so worried for me. It came at just the right time. Even though my friends and family were great, they must have got sick of me moping about.

The counsellor was amazing! A lady who just came and listened, once a week, for four sessions. The first hour I just cried. It felt like a weight off my shoulders. She was someone new. I thought there was something wrong with me. I had thought that, after a year, my grief would be in my 'OUT' tray but it wasn't. I decided when I needed to see her and when to stop. She reassured me "You will get better, but I can't tell you when but you will."

She gave me her number and said to call anytime. I never rang, but just knowing I could was a big turning point.

Then I learnt to do stuff on my own again - to deal with problems without Steve. Finally, I began to believe in myself.

My daughter and sister were brilliant. Even though my sister lives in Leicestershire, she is never really far away.

I don't mind the silence at home any more because now, it's on my terms; back then, I didn't have a choice.

I often think of some words from one of our favourite songs:

"If I lie here... If I just lie here, will you lie with me and just forget the world?"

I even found the courage to try on-line dating, but it was a disaster! There are only so many men in tracksuit bottoms without any teeth that I want to meet!

Even in my lowest times, I never considered taking my own life, but sometimes I wished that I'd

not wake up. Now, life's good - I've started to live again and have a new-found happiness in David. He's not a substitute; he's a completely different man, a man I wasn't even looking for!

Steve's family still invite us to family parties. I've been gifted another life.

Every year, at nine o'clock on 21st June, I pour a tot of whisky and raise the glass as my phone lights up to multiple text messages all saying "Cheers!" Every day now, I wake up and think how lucky I am. Time healed - eventually.

Steve and I never split up; we never even fell out. There was no divorce; he never ran off with someone else. That would have been so much worse.

I have learnt about life and the friends around me; some have astonished me, some have disappointed and then disappeared.

Should I be bothered what others think? I still think about Steve every day, but in a good way, as I smile about his Thomas the Baker's loyalty card and his love of sausage rolls.

Should I feel bad for having a new life? Guilty, because I have a new house, a new adventure, I'm creating something new?

What would Steve have wanted? For me to be happy.

I still think I can live forever. Watch me!

Gone Too Soon

As a Head of lower school, it was my job to ensure that students could concentrate on their school work without worrying about anything else. Unhappy children can't learn. Bullying, friendship issues, peace-keeping between teachers and students where I would always try to go for what was right, not who was right, were my daily bread. Years of gritty experience meant I could smooth most situations with everyone feeling valued, supported and listened to, but I was to encounter a new situation where my own life experience was found wanting.

I could sort out name-calling, bitchy pack fighting and fall outs with parents. I'd seen these, lived these, but then came a new nemesis.

Four children lost either Mum or Dad before reaching their teenage years. So unfair. Growing up is tough enough with a following wind.

I remember being devastated for them. I was the go-to giant who could solve most problems. Would I let them down today? My cupboard was bare of ideas. I was thirty - had both mother and father alive, well and at the end of a phone whenever I needed advice. Life had been easy for me. I couldn't thumb through my autobiography to find the pages they were experiencing because mine were yet to be written. I had to make something from nothing.

I invited one of the boys in for a talk. I removed my tie to show this wasn't the norm. The table had a teapot and some "proper" biscuits. Custard creams, nor digestives, would suffice for such an important meeting.

This wasn't your usual teacher-student moment. This was two sons talking together. The usual boundaries were about to become very hazy.

In loco parentis was a Latin phrase often mentioned at university but nobody really understood what it meant, in the same way people only know carpe diem because they once watched Dead Poet's Society. In loco parentis means "in place of a parent". Never had this felt more apt. The huge responsibility wasn't lost on me.

The Darth Vader who walked the corridors was on the brink of tears, pouring a cup of tea for a little boy whose mother had trusted me with her son at Parents' Evenings. I was often deemed a maverick by the faceless grey suits, shuffling their paper and poring over spreadsheets. I was never a subject teacher. I taught kids. I didn't do coffee in the staffroom. I spent my break-times talking with the reasons I did the job.

"This is SH#T!"

I swore. He looked shocked. I even shocked myself - but it worked. I had his attention. He realised this wasn't a talk about option choices, or why he'd had a sneaky smoke on the cross-country. I wasn't the Head of Year who'd brought him from primary school today. I was about to become something else, something more.

He had been sent to school the day after his Mum died, as often happened. Children grieve in different ways - they thrive on normality and routine, not standing out but fitting in. What would moping at home watching Bargain Hunt achieve anyway?

So I said "I have no experience of this, but I want to help. Have you ever played Monopoly? Here's a laminated "get out of jail" card, like you have in the game. This'll get you out of any class, at any time. If you're having a bad time, or struggling, just show it to the teacher. You don't have to say a word and then you can come here to do some work, go on the internet, have a chat or just a bit of peace and quiet. The expiry date of this card is "THE DAY I LEAVE SCHOOL".

From that day on, I kept a special eye on those children, aware that any minute of any day could rattle their equilibrium. Life had dealt them tougher cards than any of their classmates.

Children are remarkable. Friends didn't make a fuss. They helped them to belong, not as if nothing had happened but as if something had happened. As if to say "We're your mates - here when you need us."

When did grown-ups lose this celebration of "what we have in common" and replace it with "what are our differences?"

Children talk together and are more willing to take risks. Those cards were well-used - occasionally mis-used - but even when they weren't in evidence, they were kept warm in pockets as an invaluable safety-net to catch a fall.

Five years later, a 6' 3" young man knocked on my door having just taken his GCSE maths exam. He had with him a tired-looking, once-laminated card, weathered by many a spin cycle.

"I finished early. I just miss my Mum," said the voice, an octave lower than his Mum would have recognised.

Two big men's eyes welled up, but both of them just tough enough not to cry.

I hope his Mum approved. I now understand not just what in loco parentis means, but how it feels.

The most important lessons will never show up in a league table.

Back to Life...
Back to
Reality

"Right children lets rule off and put today's date..." as we put all other previous work behind us with one thin blue line.

Unfortunately, life's not so simple... no such rulers exist for grief.

Maternity and paternity leave are enjoyed for something beautiful without a hint of guilt but taking time off following a bereavement is not so straightforward.

Which of these sabbaticals is a luxury? Which is a necessity where you are often measured against the precedent.

"Well Marjorie came back two days after her sister died and she was fine!"

Precedent set. Written in stone. Pressure on.

Marjorie's shop window may have been in tact but nobody saw her stock cupboard!

So many feel that they have to return to work quickly concerned what others might think as murmurs of 'lightweight' or 'sicknote!' ring round the icy hearted. In Victorian times people were given the opportunity to convalesce getting back to full strength where nowadays we feel the need to return to the field carrying an injury be it visible or invisible. Have we really evolved or devolved in caring for one another?

We are ALL different and react to loss in different ways. Guidelines may say x number of days for a parent, y for a child… where do such poker scoring systems come from hatched in HR departments? One size will never fit all.

Life expects a sherry trifle when you only have flour and water. Workplaces sometimes offer an option to work from home - the open prison where no bells ring to signify the end of the day and 9 to 5 means very little as we are accessible 24 hrs via email and with our mobile phones. Some employers genuinely care - others appear to but then continue to turn the screw. If only more companies replaced their Head Office with a Heart Office.

Work can also be the thing that saves someone.

"Work has been a constant in my life. It kept me busy, structured, distracted. It gave me an opportunity to achieve, create and be judged on what I did everyday not what had happened to me… surrounded by friends, colleagues and ideas. Work is so much more than work."

When a dog is hit by a car they run and run and run. A rush of adrenalin overpowers it until it runs out and it collapses in a field to sleep. Then the adrenalin hangover kicks in.

Similarly so many of us send our bodies to funerals as our minds are somewhere else entirely often resulting in having no recollection of what happened. (It has been common in many of the interviews that people have no memory of speakers, eulogies or events at funerals).

The thing that hurts most is that life DOES go on. It doesn't stop. You wish it would - just long enough for you to regroup and step back on the world. It's like the piece of paper with your life written all over it has been torn but no sellotape or glue will stick it back together to make it feel like it did before.

Your leading character has been written out of your favourite play.

You may be disorganised, lack focus, be absent-minded and forgetful, anti-social, feeling vacant. (Those with teenage children will think this sounds familiar but as with those years we need support and help as we learn to leave this chrysalis stage).

Sometimes you just need one person on your side to help you through. One person's kindness and thought may shape the rest of your life.

Back in 1969 a trainee woodwork teacher had his father die in the Easter term. He returned to college but was struggling to function as the pressure of end of year exams loomed.

"Lad, just do whatever you need to do. Work as hard as you can but just to tell you… you've passed this year. I'm your personal tutor. If I say you've passed then you've passed then next year we'll get you right".

Nearly fifty years have passed since then but this warmth and understanding is as fresh today as then to the former teacher turned successful businessman. Perhaps that tutor was paying forward something someone once did for him. We'll never know.

Just to have the house empty for the first time may be the hardest part of all. There may have been time when you wanted your own space or a bit of peace and quiet - attractive when offered as an option - less so when compulsory.

Rarely are people prescribed four walls and "Homes under the Hammer" to be taken every morning with intravenous "Pointless" in the afternoon. Try and stay busy, active, involved and alive and then quiet and alone when you choose to be. Choice is everything.

Beryl had been the ever-present stalwart of local musical theatre - following the loss of her husband, as well as her wonderful family, this tight community of extended family and its values made her show go on - lippy on, hair done, front of house - best foot forward surrounded by what had always made her feel happy and alive.

It is a good idea to try and turn down the outside world volume just enough so you can be part of it but still tune into you more and what you need. Like an Olympic athlete who is tuned into every muscle fibre before a scan.

Never compare you with other people - compare you with you and how you're getting on.

"Friends helped me by getting me out socialising. I'm a good drunk - a happy drunk - I upset nobody and let things wash over me but the next day hurts on my own. Grieving is so much harder hungover."

Don't let yourself go. It is so easy for the biggest Premiership clubs to be relegated two seasons in a row. It's easy to fall down subsequent wells. Eat well and avoid blaming others - especially those closest to you who you may need on your side - its hard to hold hands if you're pointing a finger.

Everybody tells you that "time flies when you're having fun" but weeks and months can disappear if you do and achieve nothing. Sitting in your own house can be exhausting. It can be so difficult to put the needle back on the record. You may find you don't have a nought to sixty time any more - some days you may struggle to have a nought to anything time. It can feel like that first step is enormous!

Shock can act as a waiting room - a short respite from reality providing numbness at a time when the world asks for the greatest reorganisation when you are at your least organised.

"I feel surprisingly alright... perhaps I am bulletproof... I might be tougher than I thought... am I the first to come out of this without a scratch?"

Often couples have their roles based on their skills or what they hate doing - one creative and one practical - and rarely do they cross.

Many leave behind the most complex enigma machines. Infinite knots to unravel. So many questions with all answers buried or incinerated.

"How do I change the oil?"

"Where's the spare tyre?"

"How does the heating work?"

"What is the wifi password?"

"When did we buy a breadmaker? And why?"

"Why are there no recipes for my favourite meals?"

"When are the kid's birthdays?" (this is appalling I know but I was once sat down with my Dad who remembered I was born in the Brazil World Cup 1970 June... send me a cake every day Dad and I'll tell you when to stop!)

"Who do I write Christmas cards to ?"

"Can I hide behind eco-friendliness and say 'sod Christmas cards'?"

"Which lightbulbs fit where? I never knew there were different types!"

"How does the lawnmower work?"

"What do all of these utensils do?"

"What is fabric softener?"

"Why didn't I learn to iron when I was younger?"

"Do we use biological or non-bio and what's the difference?"

"How many credit cards do we have?"

"How much food does the dog eat and when?"

"Why do all those buttons on the remote control do?"

One lady in Leeds, living with MS, used her existing time alive to train her husband in every aspect of her expertise for a life without her. She estimated it would take about seven years. She is still fine tuning him with flow charts and writing step by step manuals as the degenerative condition has shown her rare mercy.

The problem is we often keep our skills and tricks to ourselves... they aren't our tricks - we need to share them. Would you leave someone you love in a mess without the things you have given them?

Sadly, you can't google "How many bank accounts did Elsie have?"

"Where are the passports?", "What is the ingredients to Nana's corned beef hash?"

Many of us comfort eat, comfort clean, comfort iron, comfort run, even comfort line dance! We do anything to find the comfort we crave that day.

Children deal with things differently... dipping in and out of grief, often seeing things in black and white. Using video games as a virtual escape like a digital Narnia - pleasantly detached from real life where energy is instantly replenished and you can continue straight away after using all five lives.

We often feel guilty when not in bits, able to get back on the horse and succeeding; it feels disloyal that you CAN carry on without them.

Grieving is like the worst hangover waking up thinking you are immune to slowly realise throughout the day your magic cloak has slipped as at ten to three your head becomes a torture chamber!

As the morning belongs to the night before, the mourning belongs to the life before.

We should remember that we are no strangers to adapting. We each have a history of evolving. We are more resilient than we may give ourselves credit for.

The problems arise just when you think you have it under control but you haven't. Like reaching square 99 on snakes and ladders thinking you're home and dry to find an unexpected snake.

I remember after two Christmases without Mam thinking we had it sussed to then find me at 8.30am sobbing uncontrollably before a present was opened. The two previous years had seemed easy as we had approached them cautiously with care and respect.

The Carousel favourite "You'll never walk alone" has the strange lyric, "When you walk through a storm hold your head up high!"

Why? Who does that benefit? Surely it would be better to put your head down to avoid it blowing in your eyes and survive...

Many interviewees have hailed the work of CRUSE counsellors or listeners as many commented - allowing them to say things they'd never dare to share with family members. Discussing problems with yourself rarely finds a solution.

Volcanoes are rarely fully extinct. Some stand dormant unsure of when or how they will erupt again because a crack is forming. Never assume it's just another mountain even years afterwards. No matter what your satnav says you may never be far from tears.

Complacency is the enemy - believing you are out of the woods thinking you are recovered. We may never fully recover - we are all recovering addicts of the people we can't live without.

Someone to Watch Over Me

Family is everything to me. The outside world is merely background hum. Life was my man, our kids and me. I had everything that money couldn't buy. Life had blessed us with the chaos of four children under eight. Every night I went to bed with an exhausted grin on my face. I had more than I could have dreamt of. Not so much a knight in shining armour but a builder in filthy overalls and an excellent Dad. There were others with fancier stuff than us - but when the door was closed, the noise stopped: that was our castle and nothing could spoil that.

On 30th March 1974 our second youngest, Emily, got a stomach bug that turned to fluid on the brain - overnight, without warning, she left us. Why us? Why our little girl? We'd never done anything but good for people. Emily wouldn't hurt a fly. I remember a policeman once looking in the

pushchair at her, saying "She's too beautiful for this world." That comment still rings in my ears today.

Children don't die. Grandparents die then parents die. That's the order it should go in. First in first out surely? It's only fair. None of our friends had had this happen. It was hard to turn to them. We had three other children who needed us. Life went on - a numbed normality until bedtime when we talked or just sat quietly with the telly off. I would go in the bath, lock the door and cry hiding behind the steam putting my head beneath the water.

We had been bringing up four children with one wage. And then we were given a bill for £287 for a funeral. £287 we never had. Four kids meant a piggy bank was a hollow ornament with a redundant slot so I had to go out to work waitressing and making beds in the local hotel.

I asked Mrs. Hodgson to pay me at the end of the summer season. I was due £240. She gave me £287 to cover the funeral - then threw in an extra £13, telling me to buy some flowers. She didn't have to do that. I remember her kindness from 41 years ago as if it was yesterday.

George was working for a builder. His boss came round. He didn't know what to say. He stood at the door without a script. After a pause that seemed to last for minutes he delved into his pocket to grab the keys to his Jaguar and said "Take your Mrs out on the moors this weekend. Get away from everything. Clear your heads. Bring me the keys back Monday morning".

People were so kind. The man from the PRU realised we were struggling so drew out our policies - not the done thing back then - just to help us. He put us way above any commission.

Our house had so many memories, both good and bad, but it felt strange without our little girl. Two doors down lived Hannah, whose son had cancer and lost a leg. She was a great neighbour. Living in that house was torture without our little girl. There was nowhere to hide from the hurt. One day, over a cuppa I mentioned it to Hannah and said how much it hurt. I couldn't see a solution.

"Right" she said "let's swap houses this Saturday! Let's do it."

"What will Bob say?"

"Oh he'll be fine. Leave him to me."

Unbelievable! The answer to my prayers appeared in an instant. I'll never be able to thank her for this relief. We just did it. I could only see the problem. She could only see the solution. We moved that Saturday! We still live in the same houses to this day. I often bob in for a crafty cig in her yard but it doesn't hurt. What an amazing gesture.

People crossed the streets to avoid us like we had something contagious.

They didn't know what to say. They were terrified I'd fall to bits or perhaps that they would. I didn't venture to the local shop for four years! I had nothing to be ashamed of but I was too fragile to be broken by kindness, questions or by people pretending to read the ingredients on the back of a tin of Ambrosia Creamed Rice to avoid my gaze.

Christmas was everything in our little house but for once the children were dreading it. That Christmas Eve the children couldn't sleep, just like many children around the world, but for very different reasons.

"Mum, I don't want Father Christmas to come. I want Emily to come back instead."

Grandparents said very little. They gave us money for flowers but little was said...

"If we don't mention it... it may not have happened." Now I realise how hard it was for them too. Nature's order hurts as mother and grandmother.

Some find great clarity after the loss of a loved one but I became transfixed on one thing. I prayed every night to become pregnant. I believed that if I fell pregnant I'd get Emily back. Looking back it sounds ridiculous but at the time nothing got me through the days more.

My prayers were answered. We got Susan. Not Emily, as I'd thought but our special youngest daughter. We had had our lifetime quota of hurt. Thank God "Lightning never strikes in the same place twice". As always, family was everything.

At 22, our Marie, the second eldest, was the life and soul of every room she walked into. She was so much fun. A teaching assistant who was universally popular. She lived for sponsored singing and dancing and making people smile. She was so kind she would go out and get gloves for the kids who had nothing.

One night after work she was exhausted but agreed to go babysitting. I didn't want her to go. She let herself in. I remember not waiting up. I always waited up. 7am the next morning our niece Karen came down saying "She's silly, Auntie Marie. She won't wake up. Her eyes are open but she won't talk to me."

Mycarditis? Never heard of it but I have now. Unlucky again. Non-smoker. Non-drinker. I was told by the GP that her getting it was "same chances of winning the lottery". Nice comparison! Some people really should think before they speak.

Marie died shortly after my Dad. I never had time to grieve for him

when this happened. I was so relieved he avoided another crack in our timeline, pleased that there was one less person to miss her.

I relived that day again and again. I blamed myself. I didn't want her to go babysitting. If I had told her to just stay home, she would be upstairs today. I blamed the man who she babysat for. It took months for this fury to die down within me. He was completely innocent - but I needed my punches to connect.

We had her funeral on her 23rd birthday. We should have been blowing out candles - singing Happy Birthday to her... not singing hymns.

We still regularly look through two Clarks' shoe boxes full of letters and cards reminding us just how much she meant to so many. I was in bits - yet there was always milk in my fridge, fags on the sideboard and washing done, folded and put away. Everyone should have a Marge, my friend from school, who never mentioned what she was doing. She just kept the wheels in motion when I wasn't really in the room. She'll never understand what this meant to me, and to us.

Six weeks passed. The house was a traffic jam of tea and cake. I had to pay my brother back for yet another unplanned expense. My cousins worked at a care home called Spring House and asked me if I'd be interested in a job there. After the first day I could have run away. It was a shock to the system but I was determined to stick with it. The owner saw me with the residents and said "You're just what I'm looking for". He put me on the top rate of pay. He saw something in me I couldn't see in myself. I wasn't going to let him down.

Having lost two of our girls, when it came to our Susan getting married moderation went of the window: her Dad said "Our Susan can have anything she wants! I should have walked three girls down the aisle and I only have one".

Not that we should ever compare, but the loss of Marie hit me so much harder. We had four wonderful years with Emily - but in Marie we lost a force of nature.

I struggled at Susan's wedding. A beautiful celebration with so much happiness, but with gaping holes in the congregation. My little grandson acted as the perfect foil to play outside and go for a walk. Family is everything.

Twenty one years on we still miss her, but we laugh watching videos of her every Sunday dinner often howling in laughter like she was still with us. Marie always said "Don't fuss". We don't - but we bear the scars.

To this day I check on my kids and grandkids to see that they're still breathing with the vigilance often only reserved to a first born child. I get so anxious when I can't see the kids and the grandkids. If I had my way I'd have all my family sat in the house where I can see them. I suffer until I see them again and know they're safe with me. I even walk up the road some nights in the rain to stand outside my 47 year old son's house to make sure his light is off, that he is asleep and safe.

Two years after everyone thought I had survived, a strange thing happened. I fell ill - sick and dizzy. I thought I had the chaos under control. I thought I was past my worst... I was in for a shock. I disappeared for three months - absent from just about everything. I went to see a counsellor: he knew all the theory, but didn't had a clue about me. I gave him short shrift and told him to put his nose back to his books. Spring House gave me 100% support. The owner Kevin apparently said "She is one of us. Her job is hers. We care here - about the people who live here and about one another!"

Gradually, I returned. This little care home saved me twice. By loving and caring I was loved and cared for: it was a two way street. Their smiles made me smile once more.

Now retired, my grandkids are my life. Family is everything. I still have a houseful of clutter, including the last clothes Emily wore and three hundred hideous mugs that Marie loved and I can't bring myself to throw them out. She loved those mugs. She'd go mad if I took them to a car boot sale. Sally was chocolate, fun and laughter.

I am an animal wounded by what life has thrown at me. We were lucky to have our girls but unlucky to have their stay cut short.

Grandkids find humour in the saddest places.

"Grandma, how have they fitted Auntie Marie into such a little box?" She'd have laughed at that as they looked at the urn on the mantlepiece.

Whenever I hear of any family losing someone at the other end of the country I phone, knowing there aren't any words to put it right. I wish there had been some for me, but there weren't, so I just say:

"Close your eyes. I'm giving you a hug. Can you feel it?"

Family was everything.

Family will always be everything.

Love every day you have together.

I do.

Imagine

I've got an idea - it's called heaven. If you think wifi or the internet take some getting your head around, just go with it.

It may sound ridiculous, but it's where people go when they die. It's sort of in the clouds, but not in space. It must be amazing, because armies of people will tell you that

your Grandfather is "in a much better place." Despite spending the past month sorting out new decking in his garden!

Beware small children, though, as they may ask complicated, probing questions. Try to throw them off the scent quickly, derailing their train of thought, as all your good knitting could be unravelled in seconds in the hands of a tenacious child's interrogation.

Completely rational people will often buy into this idea if it helps them. Atheist care staff regularly open windows in care homes to let the spirit out despite, supposedly, not believing in any of that stuff!

If you saw someone staying afloat, clinging onto something you couldn't see, would you tell them there's nothing there, or would you be happy they'd found something to stop them from drowning?

So... nice people go there, and they wear halos - even though I've never seen anyone wear a halo elsewhere on Earth (except Simon Templar during the title sequence of 60s' favourite, The Saint!)

Heaven is a wonderful place, apparently, where you'll meet everybody who has ever died. But only the nice ones; not anyone who

has ever irritated you in the past - because that would be Hell, surely?

Prince and David Bowie will be playing together, with Lemmy from Motorhead (despite never collaborating in the previous fifty years when alive on the planet). Harmonious music will be played on harps and the whole place will have been decorated like the John Lennon Imagine video.

We buy into this. Even the most devout atheists resort to "Mum and Dad are together now" - if it helps their cast iron disbelief.

I just wish they did visiting hours, or had a mobile number...

How often do we say that everything is going to be all right, even when we don't know? Heaven is unproven but for many heaven helps.

"Imagine there's no heaven...
It's easy if we try
No hell below us
Above us only sky."

For many this is unimaginable.

Bridge Over Troubled Water

We were on holiday with the kids, having the time of our lives. Mum was back in England, undergoing treatment for breast cancer. Chub's mobile rang.

"Please say it's not Mum!" I said.

It wasn't. It was my older sister Zoe on the phone. From out of the blue, my little sister had died, aged just thirty-six.

"You have to tell her," said Chub as he passed me the phone.

Chub quickly took the kids away as I drowned in a kaleidoscope of breathlessness. I couldn't speak; my ribs somehow stopped my heart from escaping. I screamed, hyper-ventilating. I couldn't stop shaking. Young women shouldn't just drop down dead, halfway through life.

We were told that she died instantly - a scant consolation.

Despite desperately wanting to get on the first plane home to be with my family and to grieve together, I knew that I had the responsibility of two small children who were enjoying the sun, sea and general frolicking of a family holiday. My heart was totally torn in two, but after many conversations with my husband and family we decided to stay on our holiday. There was nothing to be done on a practical note, and I knew the kids' world

was going to be turned upside down sooner or later so we immersed ourselves in the holiday, taking any small pleasure from watching them be happy. We did manage to keep it from them for the duration of the holiday. Lainey was four years old and Lewie six so it wasn't that hard, they knew Mummy wasn't feeling so good about something but at that age they don't delve too deeply. On top of all that we had Chubs 40th Birthday. We sat in a Spanish restaurant singing Happy Birthday to my hubby as he blew out the candles on his cake. It's one of the most surreal memories I have of that time. I remember thinking about the poem from Four Weddings and a Funeral at that time "funeral blues" by Auden, because you just can't understand why the world is continuing to turn when you are totally bereft.

The hotel staff were amazing.

I did what many people did and used alcohol to try and numb the pain, it doesn't work, it magnifies it and then you get the glory of a hangover to contend with too. I saw a shooting star the night she died, and that's the first time I've ever seen one, I absolutely buy into magic and fate and karma, but not into religion, so did I think that was Linzi? No at the time I didn't, but it was a really beautiful thing to witness and a really special moment. I didn't overthink or over-analyse it at the time, but I look back on it as a special memory.

My sister had struggled all her life, she was broken over so many things, she was the brightest, funniest, loveliest girl who deep down wouldn't do anything to hurt you, but she just struggled so much with life, she was infuriatingly chaotic, exhausting, frustrating but brilliant in many many ways.

To the outside world, I disappeared, an anti-social socialite locked away, isolated and lost. I was on the floor and couldn't get up. I thought I'd die of grief, never be right again, useless to both my children and my husband. I was desperately seeking help, searching for answers, solutions, even a miracle. My coffee table was weighed down with self-help books and leaflets, blogs, dummy's guides. Kindles, i-pads, smelly old paperbacks - I'd trawl through countless texts to find anything that would free me from this limbo. I found comfort in reading other peoples' experiences and just seeing that it was possible to come out of the other side.

It rained every day. I don't remember a single shard of sunlight or

warmth. I hope my kids forget how terrible a mother I was. They missed clubs. I sent them to school with anything in their pack-up boxes; "That'll do," could be overheard most days from our kitchen. It was a day-to-day survival exercise where I cut myself off from everyone but the tightest of sounding boards.

But make no mistake I had a small army of people that were there with me and helping the kids. Friends took kids to parties for me, they had them round for tea, and their Dad above everything else made sure they had everything they needed. So whilst I felt that they suffered they didn't. When you have children they also gift you with a hefty dose of guilt, so guilt comes with everything you do or don't do, my perspective of this is different. When you ask my kids whats the best holiday they've ever had in their life (despite going to Disney and all manner of wonderful places) they always say "The holiday with the brilliant pool and the slides" The holiday when my sister died. Their memories are very different to my recollection.

I woke up, desperate to go back to sleep, to escape the reality of yet another today. The boundaries between day and night became hazy. It was just awake or asleep. I dreamt of feeling nothing, of being at zero. Feeling nothing seemed an unachievable dream.

Little did I know what was to come...

I couldn't get myself out of bed, I rarely showered, I didn't care if I was wearing pyjamas or clothes, I didn't notice if I looked good or terrible, I was interested in trying to get through every day. Without a shadow of a doubt I would have died without my husband. He is amazing and at that time, he stepped up massively and sheltered, protected and nurtured me as much as he could, whilst also earning a living and being the best dad he could be.

I still have no idea where strength comes from. Apparently, you can lift a car if you need to. I had find strength somewhere.

"Would you like the oak or a mahogany coffin?"

"You obviously never met her! Neither thanks. Bright pink please!"

To understand Linzi's funeral you have to understand the person. Larger than life, a vivacious girl who was loved by many many people. Her funeral had to reflect that, from the bright pink coffin to the flowers, to the bubble machines at the door when we all came out of church. Even the vicar bought a brand new pair of pink Doc Martens for the occasion and wore bright earrings. We had to honour her spirit.

The last song that played as we all left was Transvision Vamps "I don't care". Almost a war cry from her, she adored that song, and it made everyone in that church smile. As a child Linzi collected anything and everything, smurfs, erasers, pens, all sorts of stuff. So when she died we made sure that she had plenty of little keepsakes with her.

The coffin jingled as it came down the aisle, there were so many trinkets inside. Linzi was ready for the long sleep ahead. Yes, she had issues and problems, but she was always larger than life and no one laughed as much as she did.

Linzi's gravestone was big and an odd shape; it was covered in Smurfs and lego models.

Her resting place feels like it reflects the life of the person at rest there. And that was important to us all. I feel close to her there, and I love visiting her.

I have no clue where Mum and Dad got their strength from after losing their youngest daughter. My mum had just finished a gruelling treatment regime for breast cancer and she was having to deal with this overwhelming grief too.

She was an absolute rock to me, I couldn't have coped without her support and help. When I was on the floor it was her that I called, when I couldn't breathe she talked to me until I could. At this time we didn't know that mum's illness was terminal. But you kind of think, in some twisted game of life top trumps, well we've lost Linzi so surely nothing else bad can happen? This is as bad as its going to get?

are scared they lash out at those they love, when my mum was admitted to hospital she was absolutely petrified. Her body had started to swell and she was breathless, she knew she was unwell but by going to hospital you know that there are going to be some things said that are hard to deal with and hard to process. Zoe (my sister) and I took her to hospital and everything felt wrong to her, the search for a car parking space, the wheelchair she found herself forced to use, the wait for a doctor, the bed, the pillows. She was bad tempered because she was terrifed. And as her daughters, we were terrifed too. In these moments when you realise all is not well with the world, and you are already damaged fractured life is about to take another blow, you do not suddenly become a Richard Curtis film, all gazing into each others eyes and talking about what a wonderful life it has been. It is raw and it is brutal It's riddled with anxiety and people saying that wrong thing at the wrong time. Peppered with moments of hilarity, you have to laugh or you will be on the floor in a heap. So we did laugh, we poked fun at people, poked fun at mum, at each other. That got

It's not to do with our age - it's the skills we have. I was the middle child, with all of a middle child's shoulder chips and points to prove. I was the pragmatic one, everything served in black and white. I was given all the jobs, I went to every appointment... she even handed me her wishes for the funeral months before.

This wasn't going to be a beautiful Hollywood ending. There was to be no gentle hand-holding or heart-warming reminiscences of "remember when we went to the caravan?" or "How we laughed that time at Christmas", with a softly-played piano accompaniment. Mum was swearing like never before - and I enjoyed the lion's share. When people us through those long days in the hospital.

As her pain increased so did her medication, so you then enter a situation where no one is really saying much, the odd comment, the odd conversation but all those Richard Curtis moments are playing in your head, your happy childhood memories, your Christmases, your birthdays.

My mum loved M&M's and I took her a big bag of them in. At this point she was in and out of a morphine induced sleep, but she woke up as soon as she heard me rustling her bag of M&M's. "They're mine" she said. She also grew tired with everyone telling her they loved her "will everyone stop saying I love you" We didn't, and I'm glad we didn't.

I kissed her on the head and we left; I didn't realise this was our last goodbye.

I remember feeling thankful for not losing Mum first. If we'd lost her first, Linzi's troubled soul would surely have spiralled her into self-destruction and we wouldn't have coped. Mum helped us all before she herself died, a parting gift to her girls.

I don't do heaven - Mum isn't watching me, neither is Linzi. I don't knock anyone with religious beliefs if it provides a comfort but I just think they live on in us. It makes me realise how great a responsibility parenting is - to bring up your children well and to pass on good values.

No matter how much I miss my Mum, losing Linzi was like losing a limb. The whole family dynamic changed. We'd been as thick as thieves; she was rebellious, ridiculous and fearless. Over the years our relationship had its ups and downs, but we were in a fairly good place when she died. In Mum, I lost my biggest cheerleader and supporter. In Linzi, I lost my shadow.

You cant underestimate what it feels like to lose a Mum. That one person who no matter what, will love you always, will always stand by you even when you're being a bit of an idiot! To use a random analogy, if you're a kite, your mum is the person at the end of the string, holding onto you, making sure you don't crash to the ground or get tangled in knots, she constantly has one eye on you, making sure you fly. When she has gone its like the string has been cut and you are either flying randomly through the air out of control or you are flat on the ground trying to get up. No one holding onto your string. It's a scary time. I'm still getting used to it.

My panic and anxiety levels told me that I wasn't coping as best I could and you get to a point when you know you have to start and face this grief and attempt to get back to a normal life. Thanks to an incredibly supportive and wonderful GP, I was prescribed anti anxiety meds. This isn't for everyone and for some its frowned upon, but without it, I couldn't function.

"Be strong for no-one!", a good friend told me. The best words anyone has ever said to me about grief. I read another one this morning "Keep standing up, no matter how choppy the waters get".

Chub helped me through so many dark days, but he couldn't protect me. He's an old soul. He was my strength for better, for worse - and it didn't get much worse than this!

I didn't trust people. I didn't want to be around them. I was fragile and hurt, with nothing to offer the world. Why would they want to speak to me? I had nothing to bring to the table. I'd become a bit of a social outcast. People don't want to see you because they have no idea what to say! I had a very small circle of friends who turned up and have never left. If you can go to someone's house when they have just lost two of the most important people in their world and say "I don't know what to say, but here's a pie, I'm here when you need me" Always bring a pie. Grieving people don't cook.

"Song for you" by Karen Carpenter still makes me cry.

Peanut M&Ms still make me smile.

I found comfort with social media, using it when I needed it. Some people are strong... some are weak. We all need people to help us and remind us who we are.

It is commonly known that you experience a big change in life after you've encountered one of the 'Big 4'. Death, Divorce, Disease or Redundancy. Those are the things that force you to assess your life and make changes.

I ventured back into daylight in late 2015. Why then? Tadcaster was underwater, flooded, with its bridge destroyed! I was needed.

I could have easily done nothing. It would have been simple. The bills would still have been paid and life would have gone on, but instead I chose to put myself into highly visible, high pressure, high profile situations where everyone would notice if things failed - and they'd know who was the reason.

Life was easier beneath the parapet. Why would I put myself through this? I don't know, but it seemed right. I think I had to do it - when you have felt unimaginable pain, you find a part of you that just wants to help people. To make sure others don't feel pain, or that they have support. It's a weird phenomenon but if you read about people out there who are doing amazing things for the world, take a look at their past, because I guarantee there is some monumental change in their life that has lead them to want to help others.

Love is clever stuff. My exile was over. Zoe and I ventured out from our rooms like Elton John and Bernie Taupin. Two sisters, separately writing the same song. We dealt with our grief very differently. I read, talked, chose therapy etc and Zoe closed herself off and dealt with it in private. We struggled to meet in the middle and found it hard to communicate for a long time, but we are now closer than ever. We each chose and found our own path out of the scary woods!!

Churchill said "if you're going through hell, keep going."

The fog had cleared. Lost loved ones can leave us the strangest gifts, tightly wrapped in perspective, giving us the opportunity to survive - even thrive - to become a better you. I value every day. I'm not wasteful with friends.

So... what have I become, now my biggest champion and support has gone?

Am I a better person? There is a guilt, fear even, of suggesting that you could possibly be better without your loved ones as it perhaps suggests a lack of respect for the dead. I may not be "better", but I do make better decisions and do better things with my time these days. I know "Me" so much more and how to get the best out of myself. I wish they had seen the woman I am today but sadly, it took losing them to create 'Me Version 2.0'.

In three years, I have gone from being unable to push back the duvet, to get up and wash my hair or to make a sandwich, to uniting, rallying and igniting a whole community against adversity.

"Kirsty is like a phoenix from the ashes!"

Its crazy to think how much has happened, and there isn't a day that goes past without me thinking "I wish mum saw that". Ironically Zoe and I were invited to the Queen's Garden Party the day before Mum's birthday. We talked about her a lot that day, and said how incredibly proud she would have been.

Despite all these challenges, I'm still here. I want my kids to look back on wonderful memories. I don't want to do well now... I'd rather do good. I don't care about my bank balance - I care what I'm doing.

Trust your gut. If it says roll around on the floor, sobbing, just do it. You won't cry forever. Supress nothing. Trust YOU and...

...Be strong for NO-ONE!

Original artwork drawn by Chub Perkins

It's A Wonderful Life

"I'm off tomorrow. I'm not sticking around for this."

And so he went. He left on his terms, no kicking or screaming. Painless!

Twenty four hours previous, John George William Dryden Bell Brown - to give him his full title - had felt "off colour" for the first time in his seventy nine years. His had been a life full of watching sport, good company and cheap beer, followed by free Napoleon brandy at our house after whistling "Oh ma darlin' Clementine" down the passageway. A life not filled with fireworks, but warm glowing embers for friends and family. A tight man with himself, but generous with others.

As a proud pitman his days were spent in darkness getting coal out of the ground, but never considered it as hard as "getting coal out of the ground."

Then, when the pits closed, he hit the roads, laying tarmac. He had an encyclopaedic knowledge of every village between the Tyne and the Tees and used public houses as his points of reference. Ambition was something felt by other people.

A character where, twenty one years down the line, the Working Men's Club regulars will still inform you that "that seat's taken. That's Geordie's seat. Geordie sits there." Not an alpha male, obsessed with hierarchy and pecking order, but an 'Everyman' who walked through life with an infectious smile, singing a song, with his cap at a jaunty angle. An enviable simplicity to his life… but Geordie never spent a minute with people he didn't like. How many of us can say the same?

He never worried for a single day in his 'one up, one down' with an outdoor toilet.

Nobody had a bad word to say about him. He adored the older sister who raised him - but took great delight in pushing her buttons! They could argue about anything - Borg vs McEnroe, Newcastle vs Sunderland… Even whether the Pacific or the Atlantic was the better ocean!

On paper, he had very little, but he was richer than anyone he knew.

Life isn't lived on paper. True happiness is loving what you have. Perhaps over-ambitious aspirants are all getting it wrong? Geordie got it right. He smiled every day of his life. We smiled at his funeral, raising glasses to a perfect life, a perfect end, a perfect gentleman.

All on his terms.

Big Boys Don't Cry

I have been charged at by All Blacks and Fijian juggernauts and come round to the aroma of smelling salts with a different profile on a few occasions. My speed and guile helped me to dodge many a broken bone, but this was a tackle I couldn't swerve. No rub down, no clunks from a chiropractor or deep tissue massage would help with this one. This was a deeper heat. Sport and a successful sales career had taken me all over the world but 2014 had other plans…

My younger brother Stuart (or "Tut Stu" as he was nicknamed by the Yachting community in Antibes, due to his Yorkshire accent and habit of saying "I'm going t'shop or t'pub") had more stamps on his passport than James Bond. As a deck hand on executive yachts, he'd crewed several round the world tours in spite of getting sea sick. Stu's 'offices' included Antibes, Monaco, Toulon, Genoa, Athens, the Caribbean and Sri Lanka; he had seen places many only dream of, living a life some considered a myth.

Stu had a very private side to him which only close family and friends experienced. He was half health food, half hedonism, working hard all day to party all night. Whilst others burnt the candle at both ends, he sometimes would take a flamethrower to his - he was never going to be a slow-burner.

Stu was on the other side of the world, in Thailand, complaining of back aches and pain in his legs. After a few months of typical male

stubbornness and losing his balance for the second time in a month, he was eventually persuaded to see a doctor at a private clinic.

The private hospital initially diagnosed DVT (deep vein thrombosis) and Warfarin was prescribed. Unfortunately, they gave him too much, which resulted in him experiencing internal bleeding. This meant they did more tests and took pictures and scans. They didn't like the look of the results on camera, so Stuart was advised to seek further help immediately at another hospital.

A few days later my middle brother, David, who lived in Eastleigh, received a phone call from his girlfriend in Thailand - she was acting as interpreter for Stuart at the hospital - saying Stuart had had his spleen and thirty per cent of his stomach removed.

He called me immediately to relay this information. I remember I put my pint of beer on the table in the pub where I was watching the World Cup group game of Italy v Cost Rica, who were in England's group - funny how you remember these minute details - and told him I would make plans to leave on the earliest flight. I would bring Mum with me; I knew she would want to be there and I knew Stuart would have wanted her there as well. You never realise how much you need your Mum until you're ill on the other side of the planet; he needed Mum - urgently.

I told her we were going out to see him to lift his spirits, because he was poorly, and to check everything was OK. I booked business class, to make it look more of a treat, as I genuinely thought we would only be there a week at the most and Mum had never "turned left" on a long-haul flight before.

We were due to leave York by train the next day to catch a flight to Bangkok from Heathrow. An hour before we met up at York station, David called me again, to update me on Stuart's condition. He told me that the results from the scans had shown Stuart had pancreatic cancer, that it had spread, and his condition was terminal. We both agreed I wouldn't tell our Mum until we reached the hospital in Pattaya the following day.

For eighteen hours, I had to lie - well, not tell the truth -

to a woman I adored. I had to protect the woman who had always protected us.

It seemed like a lifetime. There was nowhere to hide from the expert interrogator sitting opposite me; she could read me like a book, but I couldn't and wouldn't tell her the truth. She had said "Goodbye" to too many people who had made her happy in recent times - her mother, who was the centre of our family, the matriarch we looked up to, every Saturday smothered in grandchildren. Her second husband Albert, who we all loved dearly and years earlier her young nephew, Philip, who only reached his late twenties.

With clammy hands and a crack in my voice...

"Mum, there's something I haven't told you..."

"I know."

Mums know. They just do. It's their job to protect you at whatever age. No matter how big and ugly, you're still their little boy. She understood.

We reached a suburb of Pattaya and entered the local district hospital. It wasn't the most clinical hospital in the world (Stuart hadn't renewed his health insurance but never told us) and never have I missed the NHS more. This was only a few rungs above spit-and-sawdust, with families sleeping in hallways, very basic conditions and very noisy, but, despite this, the nurses were amazing.

I stayed for a week as it was agreed my role was to work on a plan to fly Stuart back home, no matter what; this needed a lot of research as well as financial management back home in York.

My mother stayed for over four weeks and made the best of a terrible situation. She astonished us in how she handled and managed everything and, with the help and support of my middle brother David who had also flown out a few days after me with his girlfriend, they tried to comfort and nurse Stuart as he gradually deteriorated and grew weaker.

Everyone thinks I'm a big strong man, but at every stage I've been surrounded by even stronger women, an army of mothers and aunties plus a wife who exceed their constituent parts.

We had to get Stuart home. It wasn't going to be easy - the cost was astronomical! - but money soon lost all value. The exchange rate and figures on a statement became meaningless as his need grew greater. Nothing else mattered.

Stu could only leave once the Consultant at the hospital had assessed him and given the OK that he was "fit to fly". They gave him the green light and, with all logistics organised, we got him back to England. The clock was ticking…

The ambulance was waiting on the runway, oxygen masks in place - next stop, York District Hospital. Home, James, and don't spare the horses!

Stuart had lost so much weight and was losing his voice too. He was so weak, but he still smiled and gave us a thumb up when I first saw him in his own room at York District Hospital.

At York, the Registrar explained that the medical team had already started running tests on Stu's condition and he would update us once the results were available. Just over an hour later we were shown to a private room where Mum and I were told by the Senior Consultant "Your son is seriously ill and won't last the night."

We were so thankful for their honesty. There were no breakdowns, no floods of tears. Mum said I had to get our Dad here quickly, and also Mum's army of sisters; most of them worked or had worked in the NHS or in care services and were fantastic support over the next few hours.

Mum and Dad hadn't really spoken more than a few words for years due to my dad's attitude even though he, by his own admission, had not been the ideal husband in the later

years of their marriage. Mum had remarried and had been very happy.

When Dad arrived, he was brilliant with my mum; all his previous bitterness had left him and genuine love and warmth was evident to everyone in the room, reminding me of a Christmas football match in No-Man's Land.

He held Mum's hand and simply said "Thank you for looking after my son. You've done a fantastic job."

At 6.35am, just six hours after arriving back in York, our homing pigeon left us for good. Did he wait for us all to be there? Why did it take something so horrific to get Dad talking with sincerity and respect to Mum again? Was it his gift to all of us?

At the funeral, Dad - now in a wheelchair - got to his feet and patted the coffin. The room fell silent. In the days, weeks and months that followed my Mum and Dad continued to speak to each other on a regular basis with my Mum helping my Auntie Helen, alongside my other aunts, to care for Dad until he too passed away the following January, just six months after Stu. My brother Dave and I believe that Stu's passing away broke his heart and that was the real beginning of the end of his decline in health before leaving us.

Stuart died with just a large sports kit bag to show for four decades on the planet. He made it and blew it! Lasses loved him. They described him as "a bloke to go shopping with, who would give you his last penny." He saw more of the world than most do in a lifetime. He crammed 86 years into 46. He lived fast... perhaps too fast. He lived the highest of high lives, always washed down with a glass of champagne. He had a shy and vulnerable side to him, but most only saw his more rock 'n' roll exterior.

Could I have done more to help him? I've got to stop this.

I have a photo of his enormous scar from surgery - it seems odd to everyone else, but it was part of him.

I have identical photos of Stuart and Dad at the races - happy, together and full of life - in both my lounge and my office. I don't know anyone else with the same photo in two rooms in their house, but it helps me. I see them as I always want to see them - like I said, happy, together and full of life.

Dave is still the middle one; nothing changed there and we're closer than ever before because of this tragic event.

But so much has changed since then... Material things mean little today; they don't make me happy.

I used to value money; now I value time and people.

Julie, my wife, was invaluable, somehow always knowing when to help and when to leave me alone, to just get on with it.

I hope I am still good company. I still meet the boys for a pint to watch the footy or rugby. I still love a good party and I still love life.

A dear friend has instilled into me the motto "Life is too short" and this has become my mantra.

Apparently big boys don't cry.

Well, I cry every day. I've never told anybody this before.

I don't think I'm alone.

It helps.

Guitar Man

Dad was a southerner-as far away as he could be and still be English. Falmouth must have seemed a world away from Hull. Back then Cornwall was just a beautiful place with dreadful unwelcoming roads... much as it is today!

He had fallen for a Yorkshire lass. I remember hearing a wax record of a conversation between Mum and Dad sounding like actors from a Basil Rathbone Sherlock Holmes film with perfect RP worthy of any Pathe News Bulletin. Nobody would have believed such immaculate diction as one was broad Yorkshire and the other a Cornishman.

It's still great to hear his voice. I am so lucky to have this. Who'd have thought a Macbook would be home to a crackly wax record from 70 years ago. The joys of having geeky kids who transferred it for me.

Dad put music in me. It wasn't just a hobby for either of us. Music was part of us. I couldn't see where Dad stopped and the song began. He never realised just how good he was. I have just one recording of us performing together and I love it. No matter what the charts say this will always be my No.1.

He inspired me to want to be as good as him. At 67 I never go a day without a song. I'll keep going until I get it right!

Dad's old guitar hangs on the wall in our front room as it has for years-handpainted in Sicily-a true one off. I have far better instruments in the house but I always go back to his old favourite. It's a dog to play and goes out of tune when it chooses without

warning but I'm sure it still knows all the songs.

I often take it out in the sunshine for a treat to practice my fingerpicking. Every note brings me closer to Dad. I can't help but smile as I feel like I'm cheating grief. Other people just have photo albums. This is more magical-it's like having a part of his still alive. I love playing the songs Dad used to sing imagining he's sat alongside me harmonising. With these old recordings and the guitar it's like he left pieces of him to help us-like he left the backdoor open to pop back now and again when I need him.

I'm not a crier because he's not really gone. All I have to do is play and he's there.In the past five years I've played the biggest gigs of my life playing to thousands. Last year I was going to play a modern song by a lad called Ed Sheeran but pulled it last minute for a favourite we used to sing to Ma.

"Now that's how to sing a song!" I was told by everyone in the rehearsal room.

I often try out new songs and smile saying "You'll like this one Dad."

I hope he does.

Thinking Out Loud

We live in a disturbing world where we can wake up to read a Facebook post announcing: "My Dad died of a heart attack last night" followed by forty seven "likes" and an array of emojis.

Doesn't it seem a tad distasteful that this is the norm to many? Can you imagine someone in the street giving you the thumbs up, or assuming the facial expression of Edvard Munch's Scream, as you share your darkest day?

Back in the 1970s, graffiti was a big issue in schools. It was everywhere. But social media isn't just a toilet wall in a school, or a tree trunk in the park. This graffiti is visible everywhere, to anyone with access to a smart phone or laptop, be they friend or foe. Think of that high street again; would you go up to total strangers and share your inner demons? Would you stand in a busy thoroughfare, chanting for all to hear everything that haunts you on that particular day? I doubt it.

Imagine arriving in a time machine from the 1970s and someone trying to explain social media to you.

"What's it for?"

"Well, you tell some friends - but mainly acquaintances, who you rarely (if ever) meet - your innermost, secret thoughts."

"So people get to read your mind?"

"I suppose so!"

"Surely this must result in some ill-thought out communications between strangers, where the cart often comes well before the horse? What sort of things do people put on there?"

"Mainly important stuff about how their life is better than yours, as well as some of the worst examples of grammar and spelling!"

What would you make of this revelation?

Like Walter Raleigh trying to pitch tobacco in the 21st century, I think Facebook could prove a tough sell. How many would love to put this genie back in its bottle? Imagine how much time we'd have to speak to those who really matter!

The omnipresent, blue and white Facebook runway lets light in on the magic, allow others to read our minds as we think out loud. Many ask you to "respect my privacy", as they instantly exchange "PRIVATE" for "PUBLIC".

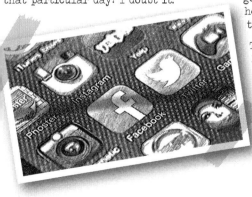

Why did he need to show us such detailed CCTV footage of his life?

In his novel, 1984, George Orwell predicted there would be cameras everywhere, watching our every move. He never predicted that we'd be the ones holding them!!!

We once took photographs of those we loved the most. Now, instant 'selfies' make up the majority of shared photographs online - a harsh indictment of who we really love.

There is research showing that those who 'spend an inordinate amount of time' on Facebook have a greater tendency to suffer with mental illness.

The virtual is now viewed as reality... the persona as the person. A world - airbrushed, filtered, photoshopped. You are Jim Carrey in The Truman Show.

But this isn't you, sharing with a closed group of partisans. Anyone can see this: friends, strangers - and predators! Nameless, faceless, dubious characters can pull the pin from the vilest of hand grenades - and nonchalantly roll them your way.

So, as with poker, boxing or war, we need to understand the rules of the game before throwing our first comment out there. You are a boxer, dropping your hands. This is 'PERSON' you are putting out there, not 'PERSONA'. This is you as unrefined ore, as raw material.

Many people take pride in announcing "I don't care what other

Rarely is the powder kept dry when the fingers tap on your commute, avoiding eye contact with fellow travellers. Rarely are people enigmatic or mysterious; instead, they blatantly turn over all their cards at will, unable to keep them close to their chest, rendering them transparent. Not a poker face in sight. This 'toilet wall' will feature people's innermost thoughts, thoughts more befitting of a one-to-one with a Samaritans' hotline. Often, the revelations are sandwiched between viral videos of cats trapped in wheelie bins, people boasting about how far they've run today and endless pictures of what's being eaten for dinner. Who cares?

An acquaintance of mine recently wrote three posts within a single hour:

"Dad just had cardiac arrest."

"Off to see dad in hospital. Hope all is OK."

"Dad has just died. #RIPDad."

people think about me", but think about that sentence for a second. If they really didn't care, would they have told you this? Very few of us get through a day without some form of validation.

Many find greater freedom within the constraints of a 'QWERTY' keyboard, knowing they can re-read and edit, only finally delivering when they see fit. Even then there is the fast 'EDIT' or 'DELETE' option, offering the hope that nobody saw their preliminary sketch.

Baz Luhrman summed it up beautifully in the lyrics to Suncreen: "Remember the compliments. Forget the insults."

This sounds straightforward but, sadly, Zuckerberg and his IT Crowd have not yet perfected the 'UNREAD' or 'UNHURT' button. Facebook passwords die with the person but their profiles live on, often causing distress to their family and friends.

For many, Facebook is the first thing in the morning and the last thing at night. Imagine the horror as, without a single warning, their eyes open to a time-hop post, delivering box-fresh photos of lost loves looking happy and alive, and asking us to wish them a "Happy Birthday" - despite them not having blown out a single candle in five years!

But is this the only way to see social media? As a place of embarrassment, confusion and pain? A blue and white runway, paved with good intentions?

Or is this view too narrow, too diminishing? Too out of touch with the world of Millennials, let alone Generation Y?

Let's look at this another way. Let's update our status…

Social media can be a superb way of paying tribute to somebody, of reaching family and friends all over the world in an instant. It can save numerous text messages and phone calls, telling infinite stories with or without happy endings.

But perhaps its true gift is to be found in the quiet hours, when the rest of the world is asleep, but insomnia has cuddled up with you for another disturbed night. You have nobody to talk to, but your mind is dancing; dancing without any recognisable choreography. The world seems a bleaker place in the dark silence of the small hours. You can't phone even your closest friend without them answering with a panic-stricken "Who's died?" so you reach out - on social media - with an attention-seeking post, hoping a "friend" will pick up your message in a bottle and save you from this loneliness with a kind word or soothing sentence.

The trick at this point is to turn this public invitation into a private one-to-one conversation on MESSENGER. This is where the true connection can happen. A connection that is still digital, character-limited, silent - but true. It can happen at home or on holiday. As social media is worldwide somebody, somewhere, will be awake to talk and to listen… these ad hoc Man and Woman Fridays would never have picked up a phone at 3am, but now they provide invaluable warmth as a chilling wind blows through your thoughts.

So, if I was to arrive from the 1970s and someone pointed out these advantages, I may well welcome this strange technology with more open arms. Without it, many would go under, spiralling downwards, revisiting familiar scenarios again and again, endlessly discussing a problem with just themselves, without solution.

I have seen the best and worst of Facebook and Twitter. When it comes to matters of the heart, if you have chosen your "friends" wisely - and that is the key to a happy relationship with social media - you won't court an avalanche of negativity. In fact, you might even enjoy the occasional big, fat, gorgeous cyber-hug.

It's easy to criticise the cynicism and needy nature of those people who change their profile picture thrice daily, so lapdog disciples will kneel at their altar in praise, but today showed me the true value of this blue and white tickertape.

This exchange was between a schoolfriend and a young lady who died but whose Facebook account lives on undeleted.

"It seems odd to be writing on your timeline, but I suppose I want your family to know how much the people who knew you still think about you. I turned 40 this year, like everyone in our school year. You not being here reminds me that we can never go back. All those people you think will always be there might not be. You remind us to love every minute with those who love us. Thank you so much for that. Happy birthday Lyndsay."

I don't think these words would have been said on the street. I don't think a telephone would have been picked to up to convey these thoughts. But he felt this was important, and I am sure it brought comfort and warmth to those Lyndsay left behind.

Surely all communication when used in the right context, where people are connecting, not feeling isolated, is useful, but sometimes small, more intimate 'one-to-ones' are what's needed.

So the question shouldn't read "Does social media work, following the loss of a loved one?" We need to rephrase the question and ask: "Does social media work for YOU in the way YOU want to use it on YOUR terms?" It doesn't matter how many followers you have. Kevin Curran, the Director of "Inspired Youth" wisely pointed out that: "1000 'likes' will never love you."

Two thousand years ago, one man had only twelve followers. One of that tiny number betrayed him for thirty silver coins. It's not about a certain number of friends you have; it's about the friends about whom you can be CERTAIN.

Love Is All Around

Sixty-four isn't a great innings for a cricketer, but Dad played tennis...

"Imagine your racket is scooping down into a huge tank of water, then bring it through the water and follow through... that's your forehand!" he'd say again and again and again as we sat through yet another coaching video.

Dad was an odd mix of big band music and anything with a racquet!

He loved that I played the trombone and tennis, but he wasn't living any dreams through me like so many parents. He just wanted me to be the best ME that I could be.

He'd rant on, and just when many would walk away, I knew the exact buttons to press. He'd get so animated, standing there in his tracksuit, but was always fit, strong and full of life. He could hit a tennis ball past me, down the line, and ace any Dad in the playground. Sometimes, as the ball flew past, a bit of me grinned at just how good he was with his big basket of balding Slazengers. I wanted to do the same to him; the apple hadn't fallen far from the tree.

"They used these balls at Wimbledon. Lendl could have served with these, you know."

Tennis was our time. Two men on court - no doubles partners, just father and son, locked in battle. He used to go easy on me at first, giving me a 'soft' set, then catch up and beat me. But by the time I was fourteen, he'd taught me too well and the one set head-start idea was abandoned in the pursuit of victory. His own tricks had come back to beat him. "Love" means "nothing" in tennis!

Cancer came along - an uninvited guest. The statue of the man with the big serve began to crumble. This was our toughest match ever - and it was to be a five-setter. I wish it had been over in straight sets, but we weren't gifted that dignity or mercy. If he'd been a boxer, we'd have thrown in the towel from the corner, long before the end. I remember sitting by his bed, watching a Leeds match, and thinking: "This isn't right. It's time to go, Dad,". Two days later he died. He gave me my deep love of music and a passion for sport, making me follow Leeds United when easier, more successful options were available. Every time I hear the Wimbledon music, I get a strange twinge of happiness, laced with sadness. It's a lot quieter watching it these days, that's for sure. No more punditry

from the armchair in front of the telly, cricking his neck round with his Stewart Grainger hair, shouting "Now that's a backhand... see how he follows in for that volley!"

I'm gutted he missed the golden age of Men's Singles. He'd thought Boris, Borg and Sampras were good, so he'd explode watching Djokovic, Federer and Nadal! Oh, and at last, a Brit breaking the Fred Perry curse! (Though he'd probably go on about him being Scottish!). I dread to think what he'd have made of Serena!

I wish there hadn't been an empty space at the top table at our wedding but, even in his absence, he got the biggest laughs as Ian did an impression of him in his best man's speech. I'm so sad that he just missed our big band concert at the Barbican; he'd pestered about this for years, but once again he got a mention and a round of applause without even paying for a ticket!

We don't always give our parents an easy ride in life, and I'm glad Dad missed out on my brush with death three years ago. My heart stopped. No-one knew why, but I'm better than new now, with bionic bits like the 'Six Million Dollar Man'. I should have listened to him warning me about the fags!

It seems so unfair that he never met Emily and Tom and that they didn't meet him. Photos don't seem to explain Dad.

Last year, in Majorca, whilst we were enjoying a wonderful family holiday, Emily startled us with "Tell me about Grandad. What was he like?"

It was as if Dad was saying "Don't you dare go on holiday and play tennis in the sunshine without me!"

Why did she come out with that? Why then?

Little Tom blows a plastic trombone around the house and has a double-handed backhand just like Agassi's at only two years old! I can still hear Dad saying "Agassi shouldn't wear denim jeans though!"

We've given an eye to Mum when we can catch her. She's kept very busy, travelling the world and assuming the role of Leeds United armchair coach, when not herding the grandkids. The house must be so quiet. I wonder if she ever puts the old forehand video on, to fill the silence?

I Just Haven't Met You Yet

To all of my friends, you never even existed. They never received the group text with "Little girl, 7lbs 6oz", and giving a name they say they love, but really they're thinking "That's horrible! How could you do that to a child?" They never saw the montage of photos of yet another ugly primate so they felt they had to say "Oh, she's beautiful!" and rack up infinite 'likes' and 'shares' to show they really are your friends, not simply someone who's bored at work.

I never got to argue over your name, trying to prevent your mother from sentencing you to a life of ridicule, nor discuss whether or not we would Christen you to appease your pushy Grandmother. We never got to the point where one wants to become "Nana" and the other "Granny", because one "sounds less ageing".

I never thought I'd be able to lift your Mum up again. She was broken… empty… hollow… bereft.

She had made all of the ascent, but was cruelly pushed from the summit, flag in hand.
No words could heal.
No medicine.
No nothing.
I'd never seen two more heart-wrenching words sit together on a page: "Born asleep".

"It's better to have loved and lost…"
I'm not so sure, Mr. Tennyson.

You existed. I spoke to you in bed. You kicked my cheek. Your heartbeat was the soundtrack of my bedtimes. You were the best piece of news I ever had and I wanted to tell the world...

I thought no-one had ever felt this proud and excited but that is of course is forbidden until you pass the 'magic' 12 weeks... then you think "we're out of the woods... it's just a formality... a matter of time until our friends play 'Top Trumps' about how quickly you will walk, talk and what an amazing sleeper you are...".

We had all the programmes printed, all the scenery built and a fairy-tale beginning planned - but you never received the ovation of an anxiously-awaited opening night. Suddenly, and without warning, a sign flashed up: 'Cancelled, due to unforeseen circumstances'. Mother Nature turned Indian giver - she built us up, only to kick our legs from under us.

Our story is more common than many realise, because you never existed... never said "Hello"... never smiled...

You, like many others, are so often ignored... but I had your life planned out

in my head - full of fun, love and occasionally telling you to "get back up those stairs! You're not going out on my watch, dressed like that!"

I often wonder, when I see your little brothers, how much they'd have hated being told what to do by their bossy big sister. I walk around supermarkets, seeing girls the same age as you would be now, and I wonder what you'd have looked like.

We have no school reports, no photos on the mantle-piece and your name is never mentioned because you never had one.

Friends kept saying "Just try again", as if it was like 'Hook-a-duck'. The last thing we wanted was to put ourselves through all of that uncertainty and heartache again. We did, eventually, but we never replaced you...

We never will... but I still can't talk about you because, to everyone else, you never even existed.

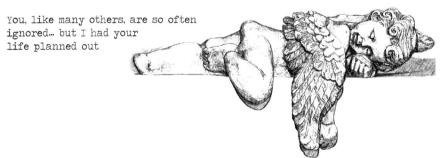

Puppy Love

Why do we put ourselves through it? We invite these strangers into our homes then adopt them like children, knowing we will almost certainly outlive them.

Why don't we go for giant tortoises or parrots from the Guinness Book of Records that will outlive us and spare the heartbreak?

Then we often have the responsibility of deciding to put them down; their lives in our hands, something we don't even do for fellow humans - without involving a clinical "holiday" to Switzerland.

They are unable to tell us their true thoughts, or describe where they're hurting, so we have to try and learn a completely new language without a single lesson. We have to take them out for walks in hideous weather - a walk neither of us want. If they can't sleep, we can't sleep.

They consider the choicest cuts of cooked meat and award-winning sausages as their right at meal-times. When we open a tin of pet food, they'll look up in disgust, as if to say "Would you eat that? Then why should I? That's not fit for a dog!"

Would we allow any other house-guest to moult all over our carpets and clothes, often making us itchy afterwards? They chew at our curtains and destroy our sofas. They fart in company, have horrendous breath and are reluctant to bathe, yet we follow them around like lap-humans with miniature black bin-

bags - praying they never tear! - and all that's without even mentioning the over-amorous climbing on our legs because "he likes you!".

I can't help thinking that if friends sniffed at one another's backsides, it would be frowned upon. Dogs have a charmed life! Double standards everywhere - it's as if they have canine diplomatic immunity.

The signs in the back of car windows read "A dog's not just for Christmas" - but it's not just for life either. There are campaigns nowadays where it's asked is it fair for older people to get a dog because they may die, leaving the dog behind!

We walk them, feed them, brush them. We even worm them! They eat every meal put in front of them, yet never once do they do the shopping, pay any rent, wash up or take the recycling out - despite them being a major contributor!

Some people love their pets more than they love other people. Man's best friend is often not another man. It's like having a child whose every medical bill has to be paid for privately and nothing is covered by the NHS. A friend of mine recently sold her car to pay a £9000 vet's bill. If she had needed the operation herself, I can't help thinking she'd have waited on a list.

The things we do for these good listeners who never answer back. And who knows if they really are listening? Perhaps they're just waiting for the fridge door to open, or the tin-opener to rattle... Where once they worked for us as hunters and retrievers, we now bring everything to them. Of all the mammals we think we're top dog. But are we? Who is really in charge? It's hard to believe that our dogs were once wolves, before the invention of the sofa. In many ways, the tail now wags the dog. Have we become one dog and his man?

They calm us. They complete us. Some people even opt for dogs instead of children. Many rescue dogs rescue their owners in return preventing them from being at the end of the care chain. Dogs make people more sociable. Dog walkers talk! Remove the dogs from that interaction in a park and the two people may as well be in a lift, desperately avoiding eye contact.

Dogs are a reminder to eat. They make us take regular exercise; how many of us would otherwise walk two hours a day without good reason? They prevent loneliness. They're the friends we want to move in with us instantly; how many human friends would you do that with? They're company, security, warmth...

They are irreplaceable. Imagine how much better life would be if people met us at the door after a day at work showing the enthusiasm of a dog!

Recently, on holiday, I saw a man with a single tattoo - a picture of a German Shepherd dog with a date beneath.

"Razor was my best mate. I didn't have to share him with anyone. I got on so much better with him than with people."

But this is not a one-way street; the affection flows both ways. Dogs grieve too. When his owner died, a Staffordshire Bull Terrier called Rocky slept on his side of the bed for months afterwards, taking comfort from the scent of his master.

In another case, following his owner's death, a Jack Russell refused to settle, so the widow took the dog to the funeral directors, to see his dead master. The dog sat by his owner's side for hours then, in his own time, slowly walked off - no words needed. He settled. It was as if he needed to say one final "Goodbye".

So, the next time somebody says "We had to put the dog down at the weekend", don't take that as just a little blip in their Saturday. That was a member of their family, someone they brought into their home, adopted and cared for - someone who added something unique to their family, someone who cannot be replaced.

I don't know of anyone who has a "dumb animal".

If Tomorrow Never Comes

Living in sin wasn't an option in 1969. When Bryan Adams was buying his first guitar, I was met one evening after work by a dour jury of all four parents who announced I was becoming a father! I was to bring shame on the family! Nineteen wasn't too young to become a parent back then, if you'd planned it, but this came like a bolt from the blue.

I was numb with shock. This wasn't how I'd planned it. An unelected committee informed us we were getting married so we did as we were told - without question. Not quite the fairytale princess wedding little girls dream of. Hopefully that wouldn't matter, as long as it delivered a 'Happily Ever After'.

Lisa was born. My little girl. My only child. I was someone's Dad... daunted.

I was still very young - a boy in a six foot plus body - working by day and playing music by night. This brought problems, but there was no RELATE back then, or even advice.

Sometimes, no matter how good a jacket looks on the hanger, if it doesn't fit or it makes you feel uncomfortable, you have to put it back, hoping it might fit someone else better.

After two years, we divorced. Another broken home. I kept in touch with

Lisa until she was three and a half but then it fizzled out. I don't remember why - it just happened. I was busy living my new life. My heart wasn't in it. Her mum got with a new man who wanted to adopt Lisa. I didn't want her Mum any more, but it ate into me that someone else did. Selfish, but all too common thoughts in men.

To avoid the stigma of Lisa having a different name to her "new" father on the school register, I agreed to have her legally adopted with his name.

All responsibility vanished in a manilla envelope. Buck passed. I could get on and live the single life, thinking about no-one else but me. I went to live back home with tea on the table and ironing done for a nominal charge.

I missed all of her school days, her musical talent, her artwork, every step of her growing up. I even missed her marriage and her becoming a mother - but I was busy. It was my choice. I walked away.

My career danced from retail to marketing to music to broadcasting. I was far too busy to remember being a Dad. I remember working in local radio when the government brought in the 5-a-day, healthy eating campaign. I had to visit a local primary school for a news feature. A lady approached me.

"I know who you are," she announced.

"Thank you."

I thought she must have heard my work on the wireless. Slightly deflated, I soon realised this wasn't what she meant.

"No, I know who you are. I'm your daughter's mother-in-law. The classroom you're about to go into contains two of your three grandchildren."

I froze. I didn't know what to do. I quickly tried calling on my am-dram background to feign illness, to avoid going into the classroom for fear that my past decisions would torture me. It didn't work.

Instead, I delivered a very poor, generic piece in which the Headteacher bypassed all of the children's invaluable soundbites. My producer was livid.

On another occasion, I was presenting a show about Children's Favourites when suddenly, without warning, "Rupert the Bear" rang

in my headphones. I shuddered and nearly stopped the show. Instantly, decades disappeared... In my mind, I could clearly hear my little girl singing the same tune; I could see her too, pushing her toy pram, a "Rupert" toy tucked under the blankets. I played three records back to back until my normal service was resumed.

Over the years, I could have found my daughter, but I didn't. I knew she was around. She knew I was around, but we never made the effort. Neither of us was able to take that vital first step; we were both terrified of rejection.

Whilst out shopping in 2013, I saw a young lady waiting sheepishly next to my car, about to put a note on my windscreen. Oh no! She must have bumped into me in the car park and was leaving her insurance and contact details. At least she was doing the right thing; many would have just hit and run. But this collision wasn't covered on my policy...

"I'm your daughter."

Was SHE the real victim of a hit and run? We hugged in a Co-op car park, not quite under the Brief Encounter clock, but with as much emotion. Words lost all of their currency. Where had the years gone? So many wasted years.

We kept in touch for three good years but then she moved away, without leaving a forwarding address. I sent emails - but got no reply. Her younger sister then contacted me, saying she'd died of liver failure, and passed on the funeral details.

I was "asked" - well, "told" - to sit at the back and be 'inconspicuous' as I wasn't "family". So I was standing, almost ashamed, at the back when of Lisa's uncles grabbed my elbow as he walked past, acknowledging me with a knowing smile.

Fortunately, I was able to talk to the vicar as I paced up and down before the more welcome guests arrived. He allowed me to go behind the curtains and have a last word to my daughter. I stood like an invisible man - hearing a eulogy from her sister as if it was an out-of-body experience, a letter saying all of the things she wished she had said to her. It was a tiny list compared with what was spinning around my head. Hundreds of regrets. A lifetime of 'What if…?' and 'If only…'.

I was angry. Angry with myself. Angry that I hadn't seen her grow up. Angry that I knew so little. Angry at being unable to fully explain my reasons. Angry at being relegated to the cheap seats, worthless, next to the unused hymn books.

Maybe I shouldn't have given in so easily? Maybe I shouldn't have let them change her name? Maybe I should have acted on my Dad's final words - "I'll not see Lisa again" - but I didn't.

I should have gone to see her. I should have kept in touch. I didn't

want to upset her applecart, or mine. It's hard to move on if you're dwelling on the past. I know what needs doing - but I've not done it yet. I know how things could have panned out - but sadly, they didn't. I barely had three years out of forty five. I missed so much - pre-occupied for the other 42 years.

If I want help now, who can I ask? All I would get would be a chorus of "You've made your bed… lie in it!"

There's an infinite reservoir of support for a good dad. Everybody wants to help him.

I am left with me. Just me. I bounce off me. Nobody else.

So what do I want from that man staring back at me from the mirror? Sympathy? Anger? Understanding? Truth? Fear? Judgement? I am scared of what he will say. Am I a selfish man who gave my daughter away too cheaply, or a man who gave her the gift of damage limitation by exiting stage left?

I need someone to forgive me but I'm not sure who it is…

I think if I could explain everything to my oldest grandchild - one of my only living blood-relatives - it could make things better. I feel that, over the years, I may have been sentenced to a lifetime of guilt without the evidence for the defence ever being heard.

I just want my grandchildren to learn from my mistakes.

The next two stories are from interviews in two separate rooms with a father and mother whose help and kindness have been invaluable in the writing of this book.

China Girl

From the start Amanda and I had something very special. We knew it and everybody told us so. After 10 years together we had been blessed with Thomas and after 12 we were en route to having the little girl who would make our little family complete.

On December 27th, life was about to take on a different direction. Hospital staff were in short supply and demand was high. Gracie, our beautiful baby girl was to become a casualty of this unacceptable situation. Deprived of oxygen for far too long... her little life was short-changed forever.

We found ourselves catapulted into a situation neither of us would have ever dreamed of or wanted. Our world fell apart and we just had to get on with it and accept it. Gracie was our little girl and we loved her so much. We weren't being brave as some said, we simply had no choice. Gracie was the brave and strong one. We felt like we were in the eye of a storm and I

Original artwork drawn by Chub Perkins

did feel for our family out on the periphery, on the outside looking in. It must have been so hard for them seeing the people they loved going through what we were experiencing. They must have felt helpless.

Our home was full of equipment, medical apparatus, we weren't just parents, we also needed to be trained clinicians. We became experts in Gracie's needs. Life became a blur, "Am I hospital today? Am I at home?".

Many donate clothes, toys and do amazing things to raise money for hospices, but they may never fully grasp the outstanding work these places do and don't appreciate their innate ability to understand what is right for you when you need them. Whilst our friends and families were jetting off to sunnier climes, we went on 'holiday' to Martin House Children's Hospice staying in parents' quarters for some well needed respite whilst the amazing doctors and nurses cared for Gracie's every need. For us, this was a life saver. We were surrounded by people who understood; people in similar situations to ourselves, members of an exclusive club that no-one had wanted to join. Food was cooked for us, Thomas was entertained. We were allowed a modicum of 'normality' courtesy of this special place.

Nineteen months in and we were settling into a bit of a routine, I was back at work and coming to terms with how different life had become. Gracie started to look around a little more, to be a little more aware. We didn't know just how much she could actually see or hear but we knew that she was aware of us and we could tell that she loved and trusted us. She only smiled a couple of times and we weren't really fully sure if it was just wind or actually a smile. We preferred to think of the latter. She really was like a beautiful china doll and it was lovely that Thomas got to see her 'smile' at him.

Gracie died on August 20th. Shock and numbness mean that some memories are hazy but I remember my sister turning up with a meal for us all, out of the blue. In times like these you really see the good in people and I'll never forget such thoughtfulness.

At Gracie's funeral, the church in our village, where we had previously had Thomas christened, was packed with family and friends sat alongside nurses and paediatricians, social workers and physiotherapists. Every one of them had been touched in some way by our beautiful little girl.

Coffins should never have to be so small. Such things are meant to be for people who've had a long and full life. At the close of the service, we hung back to thank everyone for everything because it mattered so much to us that they were all there. It seemed to take forever and we were nearly late for the crematorium. The funeral director looked really worried but it was so important for us to do.

Only immediate family came to say the final goodbye. Our little princess had gone and it was truly awful. We gave Gracie everything within our power. Looking back, we'd grieved twice, once for the daughter we had lost on the 27th December, and then again when she finally left us.

Our house was filled with cards and flowers. I remember one card that said amongst other things "Chin up" - so inappropriate, but it did make us laugh in our darkest hour. People sometimes just don't get it but I knew they meant well. Often folk say nothing at all because they simply don't know what to say. Sometimes you have to be prepared for them to say 'the wrong thing'.

I stowed my pain away and found solace in an old friend... music. I spent hours listening to music adding to my CD collection - a powerful distraction, a return to a simpler and once innocent time in my life. I would lose myself amongst the racks of HMV or the Amazon jungle.

Eventually, they came to take Gracie's equipment away, no doubt much needed by someone else. Martin House continued to support us after losing Gracie, providing support through parent groups, helping us to build our 'new' life slowly and step by step.

Afterwards 'going out' was difficult as it meant recounting a 'once upon a time' that never had a 'happily ever after' to pretty much everyone we met at a time when I really didn't feel like the most engaging storyteller. For a full year I ran on autopilot, in Dad mode; then from nowhere, the usual rational and measured 'me' went AWOL whilst on holiday in Majorca. I fell to pieces...

Following a seriously scary panic attack, I was certain that something really terrible was going to happen to me, leaving Amanda and Thomas behind on their own and in chaos... classic health anxiety. It all came from nowhere, unannounced and without warning. I'd never experienced anything like it before, so why would I understand it? My colleagues at work were great and supported me when I needed it, perhaps this was payback for going back to work so quickly after losing Gracie? It felt like the right thing at the time... but hindsight told me otherwise.

It was a slower road back this time, but with help I got there and have since returned to Majorca to exorcise those ghosts.

Gracie touched the lives of so many, one of her nurses even changed her career path in order to go and work alongside the amazing people at Martin House. Even though she is no longer with us in person, Gracie is still a big part of our home. We have a special 'box of memories' with some of her clothes and toys, the house has many photos and we talk about her often. In fact, every time my head hits the pillow at night, I know her little 'blanky' is just a pillow away ever-present under her mum's cheek.

Having Gracie taught me many things, one of them to cling on to what you've got, stick together, and enjoy the little escapes that make you happy. I want to be as good a Dad as mine had been to me.

Having another child was not a decision taken lightly. What if the same thing happened again?

In 2012, we were blessed with Eleanor… healthy, happy and delivered by the same consultant in the same hospital. (This decision was taken even less lightly). Our children know everything. We decided 'No secrets'. Gracie is celebrated everywhere through portraits and pictures in our home - very much a part of us. Her star shines bright in the sky and we all blow her a kiss on a clear night, where ever we are in the world.

An innocence has been stripped away from my life… I used to love Christmas like a kid, but the sparkle has definitely lost it's shine. The lead up to the 27th December is always hard and a constant reminder of what could and should have been. Early on we began a tradition of going to the Christmas pantomime on the December 27th, an attempt to distract us all with a smile and celebrate Gracie's life. I am really not a fan of 'New Year' either, as it moves us further away from our little girl.

There will always be a darkness in our lives. Hopefully as time moves on it will fade and get easier. I could get angry but what would that achieve? It would benefit no one but the whole experience has certainly changed me. I'm not sure how much as it's hard to remember the person I was before. One thing for sure is the last 22 years of my life have shown me just how lucky I am to have my best friend and soul mate by my side.

I could have lost her too that night under the circumstances. We have something very special which has helped us endure what would make many other couples crumble.

One last thought…

I remember being at a work event, chatting with a colleague when he asked me:

"How many kids do you have?"

"Two", I replied (very much on the back foot).

The answer I gave was so wrong. Three letters that meant I didn't have to revisit the toughest time of my life with a total stranger. I felt terrible, like I had betrayed my little girl. Never again will I answer that question for the ease of the listener. Never again will I take the easy option. I will answer in the right and only way.

"I have three children but one of them lives in heaven."

It Should've Been Me

I had just come out of a six year relationship when I met Anton. I just knew it was right straight away. We had 10 years of 'us' before growing up and becoming Mum and Dad.

Gracie was due on 27th December - a Christmas baby! Tom was just approaching three and awakening to the excitement Christmas brings. I desperately wanted to stick to our 'agreed' date so Tom could have the special Christmas he deserved. Gracie kept her side of the bargain.

If she had arrived a day earlier, I'd be just another mum today. She arrived to plan but things went so wrong. We rang the buzzer… and again… but no one came. All our lives were about to change forever - we became the 1 in 3000 statistic - a uterine rupture.

I remember being on the maternity ward and listening to a mum complain that her baby hadn't stopped crying all night - no single noise had left Gracie's lips - what I would have done to have walked in her shoes…

Day 7 they said the words - severe brain damage…. quad CP…. 'we'll have to wait and see what she does…', 'she can't swallow', 'she'll never be able to take anything orally…', 'we don't think she can see…', 'she'll need hearing aids…', 'she can't manage her airway…', 'she's likely to fit…', 'she'll need physio daily…', 'she'll need to have a gastrostomy…'. We were dazed.

No one ever expects to leave hospital without their baby but we had to

- it was six months before we had the opportunity to carry her out in her car seat home for good - not with excitement and anticipation, the usual feeling, but with a huge sense of fear, knowing just how ill our little girl really was and a house medically equipped to cater for her. Her first day trip home saw us as a family accompanied by a community nurse! We became medical professionals overnight.

After her birth, every spare second I had in those first six months was spent trawling the internet on forums to find out as much as I could about cerebral palsy, trying to filter fact from opinion. Anton trawled through iTunes - at the time, this wound me up, but later I realised these were his short visits to normality - whatever normal was - two very different people, grieving for the girl we felt we had lost and coping in the only ways we knew.

Every day was timetabled to the last minute, one at the hospital, one at home with Tom, babysitters for Tom, both at the hospital, both at home with Tom, work for Anton. We didn't have a spare minute, and this was before Gracie came home and we had full responsibility for her care.

I had no idea how I was going to cope - I had a good job, a career, I'd studied and worked hard to achieve what I had - but I was a mum and I now had a daughter who needed round the clock care. Financially, how would we manage if I stopped and selfishly, what if she died? What if I gave everything up completely and she died... what then?????

I rang Helen at Polly Anna's - Tom had been there from six months - she didn't hesitate to offer Gracie a place. I was amazed. Many would have avoided our minefield of potential difficulty, responsibility, reams of risk assessments and training from health professionals, but they were committed to inclusion and they delivered on all they promised. Gracie's key worker, another Helen, learnt and cared so much. The team were so brave and I had nothing but admiration for them.

We both had really supportive employers - with their help, and Polly Anna's, we made it work when the time came for me to return from maternity leave - 'shifts' were our life.

Daily life can only be described as a 'treadmill' - changing clothes up to four times daily, 10pm feeds, flushing tubes, medications, sleep apnoea monitors, constant overnight feeding with alarms ringing out - a constant treadmill of existence - ours and Gracie's. Some nights I felt

i just couldn't do this anymore. A full night's sleep resided in history. 'Cope' is a word that means you are just surviving. Some days 'coping' was a distant dream... we had very little in common with our friends anymore... we lived a different life.

I was asked to take Gracie to the hydrotherapy pool - a military operation of planning and execution all for a meagre 20 minutes in which I was petrified she may get water in her mouth and asphyxiate. Never again! I soon learned what was important and given the challenges we had with her weight and feeding, food was it!

There were highlights - the day I dropped a tube of cream on Gracie's head as she lay on the bathroom floor and she screamed a really angry scream - to most, they would be horrified - to me, I laughed and cried - a connection, an expression of emotion from a beautiful, strong girl trapped inside a body that didn't work as it should - she was angry with me and I was delighted - I finally had the connection I had longed for. Drying her hair with the hairdryer - she loved it - I felt her muscles relax as soon as I turned it on.

Just days before she left us, Tom was playing peek-a-boo with scarves with Gracie, whilst one of the Portage team were visiting our home - Gracie smiled - a little 'Elvis curl' but it was all I needed - our little girl was in there and she was finding her way out. This was the first of many smiles in the days leading to her death. I never got to capture her smile on film, but it's imprinted in my memory forever.

We spent a lot of time on Ward 48A at LGI - Gracie's home for long periods - we trusted them implicitly - they always sorted her out and cared for us as a family so much. She may have to stay in a few weeks at a time but we knew we'd get her back home. Looking back, that thought of a few weeks in hospital as "normal" illustrates where our expectations had roamed. For most parents a trip to hospital turns them ashen. We had become immune.

I begged them to take her to Leeds - I knew it was serious - we were blue lighted over with a doctor and nurse on board. I still wince at the sight of a racing ambulance with blue lights flashing. When they said 'exploratory' we weren't worried. They had explored before and she'd come out the other side but this time it was different.

That night, Gracie's little body couldn't face another fight. The machine was turned off. I held her in my arms, petrified of losing her. Anton had his hand on her heart feeling every last beat protecting me. He told me when she had gone.

Kissing it better was never an option with Gracie.

At 4am on Thursday 20th August Gracie left us, one week short of 20 months old. All the medical staff were heartbroken. She had fought so hard to live and had left a big imprint on all of us.

My world stopped. As before, Anton kept our world spinning - cutting the grass, cleaning the cars, returning to work quite soon after. I was lucky if I could manage making a cup of tea, never mind deal with someone's issues at work. I just sat. Once again, very different ways of coping but together - a team.

How do you tell a four year old who left the house yesterday with his sister there, to come home the next day and find she had gone? The person who dominated everyone's world, including his?

Tom started school just two weeks after Gracie died. Within a month, my house had gone from being congested with healthcare professionals, physios, social workers and machinery and equipment to nothing and silence. Stark deafening silence - I was lost.

At school, Tom's teacher asked "Can you do teas and coffees?" I couldn't even focus on that - I felt so fragile, vulnerable and strangely numb.

The school mums were a whole new world - some knew me well and were amazing throughout, others looked away, uncomfortable, not knowing what to say. Some didn't even know me, or of Gracie - handling that one was really difficult - quite a conversation stopper.

Our nights were getting Tom sorted, ironing, then at 7 o'clock the realisation: "What do we do now?"

What had effectively held us 'hostage' in our own home had been removed. But being held hostage was our structure; our life. New found 'freedom' felt very uncomfortable.

Television had no appeal. I had no focus or attention span for something so vacuous. Not even reading, something I love, helped in these hours.

We entered a short term period of "this time last week we'd have been doing this" like people do having returned from a family holiday. Our lives had been dictated by routine and the clock on the wall.

A day out with Tom came with the side order of "We're only able to do this because Gracie isn't here". Well-meaning friends said we should consider this as Gracie's gift to us. I hated that idea. I know they meant well but I didn't want it - I wanted her.

Everyone says you find out who your friends are in times of need and that's so true - it's never the ones you think it will be either. Some couldn't have been more supportive, others faded away - struggling, clearly uncomfortable and out of their depth. Some offered hollow promises which still makes me angry to this day. Please don't say something you have no intention of seeing through! It's much better to say nothing.

About a year after Gracie died Anton wasn't right - work was difficult, coping with the issues of others when he had so much to deal with himself. One night in bed he grew breathless - his chest tightened, panic, fear, anxiety, to the point he couldn't speak. I was trying to stay calm but inside despairing - we couldn't lose him as well! I called

the ambulance, praying Tom wouldn't wake and see what was happening. Thankfully, they sorted him out, but panic attacks were now a reality and something he needed to manage.

On holiday in Majorca, at a point where I had reached a stable place, he left the safe unlocked - he'd never have done that in the past - all our money, valuables, passports, all left wide open, fortunately untouched by honest cleaners. The cracks were more frequently appearing. I felt such relief one morning to hear him say 'I'm not going in today'. He had finally acknowledged that auto-pilot was no longer working. Keeping going had taken it's toll. He had three months of finding himself again and I left him to it - he needed that space - bike rides, music, building model railway houses for Tom's track - I'd had my time, it was now his.

Christmas - once such a special family time is tinged with sadness. Of course, we make the utmost effort for our children but the feeling of dread as it approaches and the memories that flood my mind during, are stuck on repeat each year. Over time, you try and create new memories, but the harsh reality is the old ones don't leave you. They re-visit when you least expect or are least prepared. A PTA Quiz night with "Rule the World" in the music round - joy to my team that they knew the answer, sadness for me at the re-collection of Gracie's funeral - her and Anton's song.

The obvious difficult times are Gracie's birthday and anniversary - further milestones that take me further away from her. If I'm honest, I also find special times for Anton and I difficult too - anniversaries, birthdays - it's upsetting to look back over the years - it reminds me of the innocence and happiness we had before life changed forever. I still struggle to take myself back there. So much has changed.

The drive to and from work in the years following her death served as a great opportunity for me to think about Gracie - to smile, to cry, to howl in pain at times, or to just hold her in my thoughts. Life gets so busy, having the time to just sit and remember someone you love is precious and can be rare.

Someone I worked with became a dad and called his daughter Gracie - he often talked to me about what she was doing, delighted at becoming a dad, but I winced every time he mentioned her name - he was blissfully oblivious, as he should be, as that meant I was 'in work mode', controlling my emotions well - he chose a beautiful name for a girl he was proud of, just like we had.

Gracie's death was devastating, and one of the hardest things for me as her mum was the thought of her being alone - my only comfort came in knowing that Roger, my father-in-law, would be waiting for her - a fabulous grandad, sadly never to see our children, but to our nieces and nephews, he was amazing. Wherever she may be now, she'll be with him and they'll be having a party, of that I'm sure!

People's generosity was overwhelming after her death. Friends

independently have run the York 10k in her memory (one twice), raising vital funds for Martin House - this is always a great reminder to me that no one has forgotten her, and that she lives on in other's memories too.

Choosing to have another baby was the biggest and hardest decision ever - we were blessed with another little girl. We were given the choice of where we wanted to go to have Eleanor - we didn't have to stay in York, but we chose to - I needed to face my fears and this felt an important part of 'healing'. I hated every minute of being in there and couldn't wait to get out - the smell, the familiar rooms, the long corridor... I know the team were carefully selected and they treated us with kid gloves throughout but I was glad to be home.

While Gracie was alive, we had a special chair on wheels for her to sit in (called a bee chair), which supported her so she could be moved around the house and sit with us at mealtimes. She hated it but it was a necessity as she was getting harder to carry - emptying a dishwasher or washing machine with a child who couldn't support themselves was bad at the best of times, but as she got bigger it bordered on the impossible.

About a year after she died, her physio, who'd I'd remained in touch with, contacted me to say she had a little girl, in Wigginton, who could benefit from the chair so we agreed to pass it on. It was strange letting it go - after all, Gracie hated it, and we knew it would be put to good use, but it was another thing to 'let go'.

Some months after having Eleanor, I took her to a playgroup in the village. I got chatting to a lady I had never met before who was there with her son - I'm not sure how the conversation came about but she made a comment to me about our children being healthy/having their health - it was so meaningful how she said it, it kind of opened up the conversation in that I totally agreed and said that I had had a child who I had lost who didn't have her health. With that, this lady asked me if I was Gracie's mum - stopping me in my tracks - I'd reached a point where grief no longer managed me but I managed it - I had it stashed away in a little box at the back of my mind, and most of the time I let it surface when I decided it could - in a controlled way. This was one of those situations, and I've had a few over the years, where it just came flooding back. We both shared a tear. It turned out she was the mother of the girl to whom we had given Gracie's bee chair - unfortunately her daughter, too, had died - we had both gone on to have a healthy child and are now friends.

Since her passing, it is fair to say I don't cope as well with change - at work or at home - I think losing her left me with such an overwhelming sense of vulnerability, that once I started to feel remotely secure again, I wanted to stay in that 'safe' place.

It is only a couple of years since we took her name plate off her door - that was the last piece - so difficult to remove.

I've never really cared what people thought/think - not to be callous, just in a way that you need to do what feels right for you - I think the hospice taught us that lesson - sometimes you can spend too much time worrying about what others think to your own detriment - it's their problem if they can't cope with it, not yours. I know that sounds callous doesn't it? My point is when you are suffering, why make yourself suffer more? I think it's fair to say you don't always have the capacity to cope with the emotions of others when you have so much to deal with yourself.

It's important to be kind to yourself when you've lost someone you love - you never get over it - I detest the phrase 'move on'. It was amazing how many people said those words to me when I fell pregnant with Eleanor - like she was a like for like, new for old 'replacement' for Gracie - it made me angry actually - at people's complete insensitivity and/or ignorance, albeit probably well meant. I'm learning to live with the fact that my little girl died - a piece of me died with her that day, I know that for sure, and I will carry the guilt for that until the day I join her. I couldn't save her.

I think grief is quite a selfish emotion - it's my grief. You can't share it. I can't break a bit off for you or ask you to carry the burden to give me a day off. Everyone's grief is different too and everyone handles it differently. Anton and I had always been seen as a couple - 'Anton and Amanda', we went together. Losing Gracie made me see just how different and individual we were - the way we felt and the times we felt them were different - respecting each other's space has been important - we take the high's and the low's and generally balance each other off well - occasionally it doesn't work like that - when we're both 'low', it's tough. Having support around you is important - long winter, evening walks with my sister where she would just listen, a tray of soup and bread at the right time from my sister-in-law - that kindness and support is irreplaceable.

I was and am determined not to be a victim. Yes, occasionally bitterness creeps in, but I don't want to live with the endless question of 'why me?' A close friend once asked me this... my answer, why NOT me? What makes me special or different? Bad things have to happen to someone - who am I to think I have the right to have only good things happen? If it wasn't us, it would have been another family - I wouldn't have wished our situation on anyone.

I love having Eleanor and doing all those girly things I'd hoped I would do with Gracie but didn't get the chance. Eleanor is very much her own character but her first ballet lesson brought tears to my eyes - she looked so beautiful but I won't lie, I also couldn't stop thinking of Gracie and feeling that sense of loss that I never had the chance to do this with her. These times are difficult, as Eleanor's experiences aren't Gracie's, but the feelings are hard to suppress.

I'm a proud mother of three beautiful children - two live with me and one lives in heaven. Sometimes I can detach myself to tell it like a story, like it didn't happen to me - some people look horrified, but I walk away knowing I've been true to myself and to Gracie. She's still my little girl, I love her and I miss her so much.

Many couples in similar positions dissolve. I know I am lucky, I have a wonderful husband and a beautiful family. He is a one in a million, I just happened to be the one in 3000....

I struggle that I escaped physically unscathed. Every parent would swap places with their children to keep them safe and well. I'd have even settled for half and half but Gracie's story will always be written in the scars. Every night I sleep with her little 'blanky' under my pillow.

What I love most is when friends talk to me about Gracie and share their memories - it's wonderful to hear her name, it lifts my day. She touched so many lives in so many ways. She was such a big part of ours and will be with us always.

Big Mouth Strikes Again

"Sticks and stones may break my bones, but words will never hurt me!"

I'm not so sure...

I was once at a wedding where the groom rose confidently from his chair at the top table and launched into his speech with a toast...

"To my mate, Dave, and Phil on holiday in Magaluf, and Jamie who couldn't miss his cricket final, and Auntie Norma who lives in Canada. Ladies and gents, please raise your glasses to absent friends!"

This happened only an hour after his bride was walked down the aisle - by her brother! I nearly choked! The guests looked on in disbelief. He should have worn a label: "Also available in clever!"

Ignorance isn't always bliss; sometimes it's just ignorance!

Apart from that particular bloke in a hired suit, I don't think people really are stupid...

I think often they just panic and hope that the words coming out of their mouths will somehow, magically, act like "abracadabra", making all the hurt and pain disappear. They're hoping they can give our black clouds a re-spray of purest silver lining, but instead this might happen...

"Oh, no! She's coming! What shall I do? Has she seen me? It's like the tense red wire/blue wire cut in a thriller. Should I stay or should I go? What can I possibly say? Perhaps she hasn't seen me... If I just cross the road nonchalantly, maybe she'll not notice that I'm a bad Samaritan and both of us can escape unscathed. Or will she?"

Remember Hal David's lyrics? "If you see me walking down the street and I start to cry, each time we meet, walk on by..." it's as if he had just lost someone he loved.

Not all silence is golden.

Many will have encountered approaching a friend, repeating again and again in your head: "Don't say it. Don't say it. Don't say 'Are you ok?'" repeating to the metronome your footsteps but then, after all that coaching in the endless walk towards them, those three words blurt out anyway… "Are you ok?"

We know it's not the thing to say. What answer do we really expect? It's 'nonversation' at best - merely words to fill the silence. Sometimes a meaningful silence would be better than meaningless words. The truth is, there are NO magic words which can heal the wounds but sometimes, as friends, we strive to find them. At a time when you feel you need people most, many of them stop calling. They avoid you, keep their heads down, thinking it's better to not roll the dice than to risk getting a double one!

The Dalai Lama said we should 'love and support each other and, if you can't, just don't hurt each

other." Many friends aren't afraid of speaking, but they're afraid of judgement and getting things badly wrong. If only we could invent the 'undo' or 'unsay' button for words as they leave our mouths. Just a five-second, 'try before you buy' option would be enough to know if we had gauged a comment wisely.

People are invariably dreadful at ad-libbing. Even the most confident communicators require autocue to prevent them from making major mistakes. Heartfelt improvisation, where a fragile audience can only accept your first answer, is a tight-rope walk without a safety net.

The following comments aren't made up; they're too ludicrous to have come from fiction. These words were served up to people from 'friends'. This section of the book is a "How not to do it". Some will make you smile, some laugh and some make you want the earth to open up and swallow you whole, they are so cringe-worthy! I hope all of them will make you think. Please try to go easy on people. None of the comments were meant to upset and most were rooted in a desire to be optimistic - but it isn't how something is thrown, it's how it's caught. Remember, it's better to use empathy, not apathy nor sympathy.

Following a death, you may not suffer fools gladly - but who does? I've never met anyone who suffers fools gladly! Your usual filter of tact and a generously long fuse may be temporarily cut short.

"You're a good-looking lass. You're still young. Someone'll snap you up in no time!"

This was said only two days after losing her husband, by a friend who genuinely meant well.

"When the dust settles... here's my card... let's go out for a drink."

Possibly the most cynical predator of all... almost with the hypnotic eyes of The Jungle Book's Kaa, as he hisses "trust in me". Hyenas would look on in disbelief at the callousness of a guest at a crematorium. Did he really choose to use 'after the dust settles'?

"I know exactly what you're going through..."

If that really was the case, would they say it? Please explain it to me, then!

"You're the man of the house now!"

This is an enormous responsibility to put on a young boy's shoulders. In the world of weightlifting, they tell you never to lift too much before young muscles and bones have developed fully.

"How are you?"

An innocent question? But then they don't even wait for the answer! They merely want to tick the box then walk away quickly, without looking back.

Any sentence that starts with "Look on the bright side..."

"Have you any other children?"

This was said with no malice, just as if Meatloaf's "Two out of three ain't bad" could be of some assistance.

"You can always adopt..."

As if someone provides a like-for-like service...

"Here's another Yorkshire terrier like Rusty. Let's call her Rusty."

This isn't like looking after the school tadpoles - but I believe they meant well...

"But she wasn't really close family."

So she didn't matter then?

"You'll get loads of cheap holidays now you can go in term time!"

Astonishing! After they had lost their only child!

"Well, at least you cleared the mortgage. I'd love to clear mine!"

This followed the loss of her husband.

"You'll be able to go for a beer whenever you like now, without asking for a pass out!"

So the previous thirty years of marriage were forgotten...!

Big Mouth can also happen with silence.

"Nobody mentions Lorraine any more. It's as if she never existed."
Sometimes, it's not just the words; it's easy to get things wrong with misjudged actions and deeds too. A care home could have given ten years of exemplary care to your Nana, but if you arrive to sort out her things, only to find her

room already cleared and back to its inoffensive, biscuit-coloured, showroom best, all Nana's precious belongings ironically thrown into a 'bag for life', it's as if a booming voice has bellowed "Next", to hurry along the clearing of the room.

If this happens, all trust is torn to pieces. Ten years of immaculate knitting is unpicked in a minute, possibly without an ounce of malice, but they simply didn't look at the situation from the family's perspective.

"We know how chaotic things are for you this week, so we've emptied your Dad's house and taken all his old clothes to the charity shop."

"Sorry about your Dad; we lost our guinea pig last week."

Not to belittle the guinea pig, but possibly not the best comparison...

"There's no amount of money in the world that'd make me swap places with you!"

And how does that valuation help me? What can this possibly achieve?

"Life goes on..." or *"Time is a great healer..."*

...and so many other trite sayings.

A good friend will ask how you fill your silences, they'll offer companionship and time instead of soundbites and clichés.

I wish more people really would "give peace a chance" instead of diving in. Remember, it's the thought that counts.

"What do you do to keep your head above water?"

This was asked of someone whose son had drowned! Yet another figure of speech used every day but, once again, it's not how it's thrown, but how it's caught.

The HMRC repeatedly contacted a widower about his wife's tax affairs 'for the year ending 2015' - a staggering seven years after her death! These calls fell on their wedding anniversary! Unbelievable. Cruel. Heartless.

The worst thing is, out of sheer politeness, we don't tell these people they've got it wrong. Are we too British? Too well-mannered? So they might even think "I'm good at this. I'll do it some more and approach all bereaved. Perhaps I'm a grief-whisperer!"

Perhaps not!

If we all made a pact, to tactfully put these people right, the pandemic of platitudes might stop.

"It's like Psalm number..."

Stop before you start!

"It's God's way!"

Then he needs to sort out his admin!

"The Lord will solve this."

Phew! I have no problem with God, but his PR team really do over-promise and under-deliver.

"Well, she was never really born, was she?"

So she never happened? Sorry to have bothered you!

"Yes, but £248,000 is a lot of dosh! That's like question 10 on 'Who wants to be a Millionaire!'"

Sometimes, honesty isn't the best policy with those closest to us. The truth can really hurt if served neat. To quote Jack Nicholson in A Few Good Men... "You can't handle the truth".

Many of us can't. One father of three, having lost his wife of over thirty years, announced "Kids, you're NOT enough!" If given his time again, would he still have said this? It was a spur of the moment, wounded comment from a desperate man. Four words, said in haste, that will echo forever.

"He's in a better place..."

Without us, AND he'd just got a new conservatory!

"If you think it's bad now, it gets worse!"

Thanks!

"That which doesn't kill you, makes you stronger!"

Shall we play 'football manager's post-match comment bingo'?

"God needed one more angel in heaven."

He must have millions by now! We only had one little girl!

"The Lord moves in mysterious ways..."

"He did this because he knew you were strong enough."

So it's my fault? I wish I'd been weaker.

"I'll tell you what you're thinking..."

That's Derren Brown's act nicked!

"Only the good die young!"

My Nana was a hundred and three, and she was fantastic!

"I've set you up with Tom from work. He reminds me a lot of Phil, but he's not as tall."

Means well, but do I look like I need a stunted double of my husband?

"How could anybody leave their kids?"

Suicide. Judged!

"I lost my daughter 2 years ago."

"Well, you should be over this by now."

There was outrage when a solicitor said this... (I was brought in to write a bespoke bereavement course for care staff to help support families).

"Would you jump in my grave as quickly?"

Beware of making colloquial comments when people steal your seat; they could be heart-breaking...

"You'll know about this, you used to be a Dad too."

Said, carelessly, after too many beers, where thought was detached from the conversation.

"I sent Marian a beautiful bouquet when Kenneth died and did I get a 'thank you'? Not a word!"

Astonishing!

"Put it behind you… move on."

"Man up, fella. Lasses cry!"

"What's with the big daft tattoo?"

Do you mean the personal tribute to his late mother?

"Right, children, today we're making Mother's Day cards…"

Despite two children in the class no longer having a mum… (It's not as easy as "Today we're making Parent or Guardian or Significant Other cards". They might run out of PVA glue and glitter…!)

"There's been an 'RTA', Madam."

What's an 'RTA'? Another 'TLA'! A three-letter abbreviation for 'Road Traffic Accident' - but this is NOT the time for jargon!

"Cheer up, mate, it might never happen!"

Too late, I'm afraid.

"If Dad was here, he'd let me go to the party. I wish he was…"

A harsh, low blow.

"Have you or your family had an accident in the past three years that wasn't your fault?"

Yes, but the outcome is clearly NOT on your database!

"Would you like to try some perfume for your wife?"

Nothing meant… the probability is a man of that age IS still married.

So we need to actively listen - listen to every word, and take a second to process, before answering. How often do we plan our next sentence while we're still only halfway through listening to what someone is saying? Take a second, 'taste' your words before serving them up to others. Without thought, they might be poisonous!

Remember that we have two ears, but only one mouth. Why don't we use them in those ratios? You'll surely never hear anyone say: "Me and my big ears! I wish I didn't listen so much!"

Avoid playing the album: "Now That's What I Call Platitudes".

I hope this "how NOT to do it" guide has been helpful and just remember… "A closed mouth gathers no foot!"

I Don't Wanna Talk About It

It's difficult to read minds at the best of times. Imagine how much harder that becomes when someone isn't sure what is going on in their own heads?

Conversation can be difficult, stilted and awkward. This could be a time where you are afraid to go near. Please refer to the "Big mouth strikes again" chapter to explain how NOT to do things.

Words don't always come easily. Sometimes people need time and space. Time to process what has happened and an egg timer rarely fit the needs of the individual. They may not want to talk. Everybody is unique. You don't know what to say or how to help.

"Call me if you need anything" may not work. It might just let you off the hook and if they never call you think:

They are fine

You, in some small way, helped!

Hoping that the next time you meet, time will have healed their wounds and you can have a normal conversation again, as if nothing ever happened. Surely that is ridiculous! That would never happen... But this will be happening to many friendships all over the planet today. So how can we avoid this "as you were" approach?

In truth, few are the friends you could ask to deliver on their promise. We need to be expert shop assistants and read our customers - decide whether they want us to approach and help them or just leave them to it. It is a balancing act that takes skill and empathy.

"Even at the bereavement support group, I don't know how to be with people. We all know why we're there so don't need to ask but I wish people wore a smiley face or a sad face to explain whether they are wanting to be optimistic or wallow forever like Queen Victoria."

If you struggle with words, actions can make such a big difference.

"I'm just off into town - what can I get you from the shops?" suggests you are already going so nobody feels like a burden - that dreaded word worn like a millstone for people grieving.

"I was baking brownies, so I did a few more. I thought you might like them with a cuppa. I'll stick the kettle on" - once again, this suggests you were already doing something, so it has not been done especially for them (even if it was).

"I've tried a new recipe and made too much shepherd's pie. It can be

frozen if you've already sorted out dinner" - nobody will ever find fault in such generosity.

"Would you like me to bring Luke home from football tonight? I'm already picking my two up. He could come to ours for tea after school as well, if you like." Practical offers like this can make such a big difference to a parent juggling a complex calendar single-handedly.

Using humour in the right measure and at the right time can help.

"Let's go outside put on the gloves - go heavy to the body, light to my face and get this out of you..."

Thankfully, this has always raised a smile; nobody has taken me up on the offer yet. But it highlights that I will do whatever they need to help.

You can help your friends help you by writing a letter. They may be lost in need of your direction. You probably couldn't tell them face-to-face, but you can be much more focused in a letter.

Edward Bulwer-Lytton wrote: "The pen is mightier than the sword."

This could be the key to success, the catalyst to togetherness.

Nobody writes letters any more since texts and emails replaced them.. "snail mail" is deemed an outmoded medium but it could make the difference. Remember who the true victor was in the Tortoise and the Hare.

We are fearful of grammar and punctuation pedants. We get hung up that we've forgotten how to set out a letter. Where do I put my address? Am I faithfully or sincerely? Could it even be 'luv n hugs'?

Hopefully by the end of reading it they will realise that you are FAITHFUL and SINCERE.

Forget these and realise just how special a letter makes you feel... not in an elaborate font but in your own quirky handwriting. A connection of ink and paper that can reach the heart so much better than any text, voice message or email and can be revisited again and again. It shows you have bothered. It shows you are bothered.

Even the gaps between the words punctuate the care you have taken providing a series of safety nets. The words YOU MATTER permeating throughout. Those pages may be read years afterwards, to see how far you have come, documenting your survival. Not an emoji in sight. If you need to use an emoji, you've not used the right words. I'm sure the inventor of the semi-colon never thought "One day I'd love this to be tipped on its side as if I'm winking."

Some things are well worth your time and effort. A letter is private between writer and recipient - it's not for public consumption. It is not a sympathy card with generic rhyming couplets written by a failed poet paying the bills by doing something she doesn't believe in. If someone you love has died, you can open your heart without falling to pieces and explain how you are and what you need from your dearest friends, without going off on tangents or dissolving like a pair friends watching "Beaches".

You can say what you need and what to avoid.

"Dear Sarah,

I'm in bits but please keep calling me. I might have the phone on answer machine to screen my calls but please leave a message. I'm still me - just a fragile, brittle version. My head's a shed so if I say something stupid, please forgive me. Nothing is meant. I value and need friends like you more than ever. I don't want you walking on eggshells. I'm OK so long as people aren't too nice to me. Still have a laugh and take the mickey out of me as you always have. Please don't be afraid to ask me about Dad. I want to keep him close. This might help. I might fall to pieces occasionally, but I'll be fine in a minute. Allow me to be me and you be the best friend I have always had.

Show me I belong. This is the toughest thing I've ever had to deal with. I don't want to do it alone.

If I keep turning down nights out, please don't stop asking. I will come out when I am ready. Thanks for walking beside me through everything life throws at me. Love you.

Thanks."

Sometimes even finding an envelope or a stamp may be overwhelming following a recent bereavement, so these words in an email or text may suffice and be more manageable for some.

Asking for help and being honest can work wonders. I was teaching a group of 15-year-olds in a pupil referral unit for permanently excluded students on the day my uncle died. I was upset but had to go in.

"Fellas I've lost my favourite uncle today. It's not great. Can we have a good day today?"

They were superb. Kept busy all day. Not a sound then at the end of the day, one lad came up and said: "Hope you're all right, sir."

Honesty proved to be the right policy.

If you are the friend of someone grieving, say what you are afraid of, the mistakes you are terrified of making, how you are anxious about messing up. This honesty will be refreshing... it highlights your weaknesses but also your respect and love of the person and how much their friendship matters to you. This will help you and them sharing hope, expectations and respect.

Nobody will ever mark you down for poor spelling. They will know you are there for them and they will never be alone. Togetherness and belonging is vital. The power of the wolf is the power of the pack.

Loneliness, isolation and exclusion will hate these letters. That's what friends are for so become the friend you would love to have. One of these letters in an envelope could cement your friendship forever.

"Only those who really care about you can hear when you're quiet".

The best thing you can offer is relief, reassuring them you are there removing any fear.

"Lean on me
When you're not strong
I'll be your friend
I'll help you carry on
For it won't be long
Til I'm gonna need
Somebody to lean on" - Bill Withers

Nominate someone not too close to you to cascade information to people. Like an efficient personal assistant to act as your filter, organiser, bodyguard and human shield to protect you from things you don't need to get involved with. You have far bigger fish to fry. You may not want to reiterate yet again. Choosing the right person for this role could be the key to your early survival and allow you space to think, talk and reflect with those who really matter.

There are other letters giving permission or a blessing for the future…

One husband wrote a letter of "permission" for his wife to remarry so long as he wasn't too good looking and funnier than him! "Go for a rich man next time…"

You may be surprised… like voices from the grave. Not a Dear John letter but a "you deserve to be happy letter" could pave the way for the rest of your life.

Sometimes you may be the best motivator. Advice is easier to give than to receive. This idea may seem odd but has helped many people since I suggested it.

On a good day when you are thinking clearly and positively, record a video blog or set your Dictaphone running as you are out walking the dog explaining WHY it is such a good day, what you are thinking and how you are feeling so that when you aren't as coherent you can play this back to coach yourself. It will almost feel like someone else but with your face and voice - you know this person well and trust their advice.

These could be just the words of encouragement and motivation you need on another day coming from a familiar face. You can become your own motivation.

Also record yourself on a bad day and comment why you are struggling. This may prevent mistakes being made twice. It can allow you to learn from yourself and see just how far you have come when looking back.

Keep a journal/diary on your bedside table and write as much as you can (not online - sometimes it is better to keep your inner thoughts to yourself). We forget so much, reflection could inspire a change, we can learn so much from us plus time. Diary entries will be littered with repetition, but you can see the tides ebb and flow from anger to thanks to acceptance.

We can use our past and present to help shape and improve our futures. You may not recognise the person who originally wrote your diaries, and that is when you know change is happening.

Over the years, I have seen many friends go through hard times and wondered how I could help. I sat and listened to them and offered advice only when asked, and then started sending them regular text messages on a morning and at night asking them to self-assess "How many out of ten" they felt at that moment.

This can serve in many ways. Initially, it's a subtle suicide watch that they are alive and well and haven't done anything reckless. Then it shows there is somebody out there who cares; but its real worth comes about when they tune into themselves and know what a 4 feels like or what an 8 feels like and more importantly how to turn a 4 into an 8. They will then pre-empt a bad day and put measures in place to distract or improve things with appropriate activity or inactivity.

It's all about tuning into them and empowering them to take ownership of how they feel. This system starts off daily but then becomes an "as and when" system. Eventually people don't need me because they automatically say "I'm a good 8 today" or "I was a bit of a 4 last night but today's an easy 7 and a half!"

I have asked some friends to write a letter to the person whom they have lost. They have found that difficult initially but uplifting, moving and released some beautiful memories they had long forgotten. Taking the time away from gadgets to sit and write is beautiful.

I asked my Dad to write one for my mother - he told me it really helped. He sat there for ages looking over old photographs going through happy memories then he put pen to paper, put it in an envelope and sent it to me.

"Dear Alice,

Thank you.

All my love

Charlie

Xxx"

Eight words summed up 42 years together perfectly.

Telling someone something wonderful their absent friend did for you or what they meant to you can also prove valuable. Share what YOU miss about them from a different perspective but

Don't make it about YOU!

Are these ridiculous little ideas?

Not if they work for you.

If you are one of these...

SILENT

...you can do the other

LISTEN

Substitute

"I'm sorry, Madam, but the fillet steak is off. May I recommend the sirloin?"

"Yes, that'll do."

This innocent exchange got me thinking...

Is there a finite amount of happiness in the world? In order for a champion to have his gloves raised aloft, does the other man have to be on the canvas? If it lands on red, black loses. I often think about this. Have I stolen someone's happiness? Have I taken someone else's life? Am I wearing a Dead Man's suit ?The feeling of guilt hangs over me without reason, guilty without ever committing a crime.

Am I am only here gazing at her, because my predecessor took a corner too quickly? Are my roses worth as much as the lilies rotting in the rain, watching over the deadly bend? Is this really my role, or am I the understudy nobody paid to see?

I'm only here because someone else isn't. I wouldn't have been noticed or needed. I would've still been sitting on the substitute's bench - my squad

number well above eleven! - as she grew old with her first love, first teamer.

Any other bloke can mess up and have an off night, but I'm in a ménage-a-trois where I can't compete; three in a bed, where I often have to roll over to make way for a better, kinder, more considerate version of me; a predecessor, with all warts removed, airbrushed and regarded through eternally rose-tinted lenses. If I mess up, like any normal guy, I can be beaten with the stick... "Rich would never have done that!", "Rich and I loved Ibiza...", "Rich used to play that on the piano...", "Rich bought me this...", "Rich was so kind!"...

It's hard to compete with a ghost.

I didn't steal her from him. It wasn't my fault. Why must people insist on playing judge and jury, even if their judgements sentence someone to a life alone?

Her friends don't like me - not for being me, you understand, but for NOT being him.

I wish they'd just ask:

Do I make her happy?

Does she deserve to be happy?

Lucky I showed up.

I came along as a replacement.

Am I "Mr. Right", or just "Mr. Right Enough"? Am I here for love or company?

The words of Crosby, Stills and Nash ring out in my ears: "And if you can't be with the one you love... honey, love the one you're with."

But I always have this niggling question in the back of my mind - even five years after he died, if he could somehow walk through the door today, would she stay in my arms - or run to him?

I'm Still Standing

"You'll never guess who's dropped down dead..."

Audrey uses this as an opening gambit to virtually every conversation. She then tells you a lady's first name, but omits using a surname you may have had a chance of recognising, using instead her maiden name from 1957! If I'm being honest, her social life is dictated by the obituaries column. I'm sure she would fill the "Hobbies & Interests" box of any pro forma with "FUNERALS".

Very few weeks go past without her skulk of silver foxes venturing onto icy pews, singing at the top of their voices, celebrating that their numbers are, as yet, uncalled. Almost addicted to the strangely welcoming aroma of damp hymn books, "The Old Rugged Cross" is virtually sung on a loop. But these funerals are not a festival of doom and gloom:

they are celebrations of absent friends, opportunities to be together and "belong" for the season-ticket holders in the local churches and chapels. Each week is like another episode of "COME DIE WITH ME" as they compare flowers, buffets, Swiss rolls and eulogies.

I often ask my Dad, now 81, how he is.

"Well, I checked in the newspaper this morning - and I'm still alive!"

Behind this veil of humour, though, is a sadder tale. On many days, the newsprint features familiar names - men he's worked with, bowled at, laughed with, sworn at. Men he's shared years with - all gone. Reading an obituary to me, his reluctance to reveal the age in turn reveals it is probably less than his.

The music stops and yet another chair is removed. The now slower-paced dancing resumes, often with Zimmer frames and walking sticks. In this war of endurance, could he be the last man standing?

Where once there was a full auditorium who knew his act inside out - stories, jokes and songs - the attendances have slowly dwindled. His act is still as funny and engaging as ever, but the roar of the crowd has faded to a whimper. There are fewer people now who know the stories, know the man, his history, his memories, his victories, his defeats.

What is the prize in this lifelong game of musical chairs, where younger, fitter participants have often left early with their party bags?

He will be left sitting in an empty room, on the last chair, without anyone to remind him who 'Charlie' is.

Without meaning to, 'Charlie' could disappear - people will know him only as Dad, Grandad or Mr. Donaghy.

But despite the reality of seeing so many friends exit, his attitude is still about enjoying every today - and every tomorrow.

"Growing old is rubbish, but it's so much better than the other option, so I'm going to get to a hundred first, have a cup of tea... then see how I get on from there!"

Still standing.

Who's Next?

As I write this, the world clambers to the end of 2016 wondering who will be next? It seems like the Grim Reaper has rifled through our record collections and childhood heroes and knocked at all of their doors.

Is 2016 any different to any other three hundred and sixty five sunsets? The population of the world isn't dwindling - people die, people are born every second - but in 2016 the focus has been on the mass exodus of some of our favourite strangers.

Huge outpourings of emotion for people we have only encountered in two dimensions fill every column inch. We 'shush' our loved ones on sofas so we can hang onto these strangers' every word, even if they aren't actually their words and are being read off autocue! We'd always keep our appointment with Top of the Pops, despite turning up late for more important occasions.

Our pin-ups have become obituaries. The media have, over the years, placed these people on pedestals, turning them into stars, immortals fit to live next door to Zeus but with bigger cars! We mourn them because of the bits of our lives they have taken with them.

It's not who they are. It's who they are to you.

The stark truth is we are getting older. We are not the age that we think we are in our heads. No matter how much Botox we inject or how many visits we make to various fountains of youth, we are the age of our necks and the backs of our hands! In reality, no matter how many Instagram followers we have, we are all made from the same bits!

Once, we would sit down at the end of a busy day to catch up with world events on News at 10, to see what was worthy of the bongs. Then at the end of the bulletin, instead of going to an "And finally..." story about a squirrel that could water-ski, a picture would appear of an actor who used to be in films years ago, or an author who wrote a book you

Twenty-four hour Twitter is used as CCTV to stalk celebrities with their consent as we adopt the bizarre title of "followers" - a mere stone's throw from the word "disciples"! We see a name and a hashtag and instantly think they've died, as what else could they have done to be in our consciousness today? To topple #bakeoff , #brexit or #trump from the hashtag top spot?

As soon as the announcement of a celebrity death is made official, the internet ignites with total strangers writing personal, heartfelt eulogies linked to youtube videos for people they have never met, yet felt they had shares in.

The media instantly turns hypocrite, never speaking ill of the dead. The BBC omits to mention they dropped Wogan like a stone for a ground-breaking Spanish drama called Eldorado; George Michael is deemed a national treasure and iconic songwriter where once "Zip me up before you go go" had peddled their red tops! Yet they still print a picture of him just before he died. Why?

We are in danger of losing all dignity and thought for these people and their families. One paper mentions "Victoria Wood's secret cancer battle". Surely the word should read "private"? She never kept a secret from the world. The sentence speaks volumes about expectations and access to people in the public eye.

were forced to read for 'O'-level English, followed by "...died today aged 81" - and we DIDN'T know about it!

Such a time did exist. We got through the whole day without knowing someone had died. Can you imagine? It seems a distant memory, like not smoking in pubs, or couples talking to one another in restaurants without taking photos of their meal! Once upon a time, we knew nothing until Trevor Macdonald told us.

Now the "news" isn't. As newspapers document what happened yesterday, television news plays a similar role; John Snow has been superseded by tickertape teleprinters of unequal measures of fact and opinion in our pockets.

Why does the reporter need to be outside the deceased's family home? Imagine, following the loss of your mother or father, the ever-empathetic Kay Burley from Sky News reading autocue outside your front door.

Why does the grieving widow have to talk to Lorraine Kelly?

Why do we need to know how much their estate was, and who it is being left to?

Why do we need to know the finer details of post mortems? At what point did we all become Quincy?

Why are photographers with long lenses allowed and welcomed at funerals to zoom in on the worst moment of their life?

I remember being appalled in 1997, sitting alone and watching the funeral of Princess Diana, shouting

at the television screen "get your cameras off the lads' faces! That's their Mother!"

Then a stark reality hit me. Perhaps I was the reason for that close up? To tug at my heartstrings and turn the screw to open the floodgates?

Are we the reason this sideshow exists, like a convoy of nosy motorists, uncontrollably rubber-necking, unable to avoid gawping at the crash that selfishly 'ruined' our journey?

If I watch, if I buy the newspapers, if I read all the posts on social media, perhaps it's not their fault.

Perhaps it's mine.

Our House

After ten years, I'd recently moved house without any emotional attachment. It had seen us married and have two children, but we'd just moved down the road to gain an extra bedroom and pay another £90,000 to remove the word "semi" from its description. Clearly, moving house was no big deal, so I agreed to help Mum downsize.

It was thirteen years since Dad had died but we knew we always had home to go back to. Layers of our past were peeled away to reveal dubious DIY projects and shadows of where pictures once hung. Old tennis rackets and 'vintage' trainers littered the cupboard under the stairs. I don't know what our hall smelt of, but every time I opened the door it hit me as if I was still running in from school, shouting "I'm home!" How much would I pay to have that unique fragrance bottled years from now?

This wasn't a 'property' like it read on the estate agent's brochure, with soulless, inoffensive elephant's breath paint in every room. This 1960s' semi was a museum of "us", where nothing had ever been thrown away. The piano stool overflowed with over-ambitious sheet music that would never be played to the standard Dad had hoped. VHS cassettes lined the wall like an

intellectual's library, years after the video recorder had retired into the garage that never saw a car.

This was the café where I could always come to be spoilt by Mum, to enjoy an oversized, agricultural portion of apple pie - which justified using the last hole on my belt - before driving home. Being fussed over never lost its appeal, even as it met with our wives' "tuts" of disapproval as they refused to follow suit.

The house still echoed of Christmases past, birthday parties, arguments and laughter, big band music and the constant hum of football crowds on the telly. Outside, the garden stayed unkempt as the fastidious groundsman had left, never to be replaced. I can almost see kids, with scuffed knees, moving homemade cricket stumps to

fortune to fill. "Could do better" school reports from decades ago were thrown into bin bags. 500-metres breaststroke badges, fridge door masterpieces and home-made Mother's Day cards - now just junk. I should keep them, but they'd only clutter my house. One man's junk is often another man's junk too!

Today hurt more than I ever thought it would. I thought I was just helping Mum move into her new flat. Gone are the echoes of "get up to your room!" - but the good memories are gone too.

Saying goodbye to Dad was heart-breaking. I thought I had at least finished with that, but now I realised I still had him at hand, his stuff surrounding me as it always had. That faint aroma of stale aftershave was engrained into the Draylon of the settee as if he was still there. This was his home, my home, our home. The place where we always felt safe, where nothing could hurt us, even after he left.

I was fine seeing the 'FOR SALE' sign and discussing how much fun the equity could give Mum, but the problem of a house in a sought-after area is that it soon becomes a 'SOLD' sign. It dawned on me that this was a proper goodbye.

Goodbye for good. The only way I would ever get to see these rooms

avoid Raleigh Choppers and Grifters, racing to the out of tune ice cream van where we always asked for a "99", smothered in monkey's blood! I can see where once Dad proudly polished his Austin Montego taxi that could speak like Knight Rider - until he had it deactivated as it drove him mad, telling him to put his seatbelt on!

"She's not telling me what to do! That's your Mum's job!"

But today was a different visit, far worse than the funeral procession. Today, all of our history has been mummified in newspaper and put into boxes marked "keep", "junk", "carboot", "ebay" and "charity shop". Off to places where people buy 'junk' but strangely sell 'antiques'! Lego, Action Man, Sticklebricks, Downfall and old Pannini sticker albums - filled with an array of footballers' moustaches and perms - that cost a again was by closing my eyes and hoping they were still with me. I hoped my memories would never fade.

This "two bedrooms and a box" witnessed my every stage from toddler to father of two. It put up with some of the worst trombone and clarinet playing known to man! It kept us safe and warm and we never once said "Thank You". Mum had been rattling around in it for a decade. It was eventually too much work and hassle and she'd prefer to be nearer to town - maybe even go on more holidays!

I bent down to carry a lifetime of memories into various vehicles, then looked back at the stark, cold hallway. I clapped to hear its empty echo slap back at me as I turned the light off for a last time.

"Goodbye little house… I'll miss you."

A final goodbye.

I dropped Mum and the keys off, waited until the door had closed, then I cried like never before. I never saw it coming. Mum and Dad had worked so hard and often struggled to give us our family home, but now it was just a folder on a shelf, another 1% commission for an estate agent. That pot of golden equity might create many new memories for Mum but one thing is clear… houses are so much more than a pile of bricks.

I have just been downsized.

These Foolish Things

"A champagne glass that bears a lipstick's traces

An airline ticket to romantic places

Oh how the ghost of you sings

These foolish things remind me of you"

These beautiful words written by the little-known Eric Maschwitz perfectly sum-up both the comforts and stumbling blocks for those left behind: the foolish things. The little things.

Like a legion of King Canutes, we attempt to stop the tide but often end up drenched. If you have spent many years with someone then just about everything you encounter in your day-to-day life will be linked to them in some way. There is no escape.

Sometimes, without warning, something will creep up on us and infiltrate one of our senses. Whether they're through music, food, smells, phrases, a television programme or even a quirky mannerism, these reminders can reduce the crustiest of loaves to breadcrumbs. Nothing is off limits.

These constant reminders can hurt or heal. As one interviewee said of his home, "The problem with this house is the memories. The best thing about this house is the memories. I could never leave them." Often crying and laughing do share common borders. After both crying and laughing, we can feel alive, cleansed or re-booted - a human version of "switch it off and switch it on again".

You get up; brush your teeth and prepare to face the day ahead. No warning is given. No clouds to be seen in the sky yet at some point something will hit you - a bolt from the blue that takes you back to a precise moment in time. Whether it's Brut and Old Spice on a pillow or those photo albums covered in tear-proof polythene with hideous padded covers, they can make you laugh or make you cry. Either way, they remind you that you feel. The smallest of things can have the biggest impact. OXO cubes make my Dad crumble - "How bloody stupid… something as harmless as OXO cubes!"

A song on the radio can force you to pull over to re-apply your mascara as Celine Dion has made you resemble a panda. While driving, you may find yourself following the less-painful diversions of your own creation in order to avoid a particular landmark or emotional road-block. Even while walking, I'm sure we've all been caught off guard when following a back-of-the-head doppelganger. You may know full well that they're not the person you long to see but you still walk a little quicker to check from the side and front that they haven't faked their death and left their clothes on the beach like Reggie Perrin.

Rather than taking us aback, we can find ourselves clinging to these small triggers... Dad had always changed his car every two years for yet another uninspiring lacklustre A to B mobile with a 1300cc engine. From Morris Marinas to Chrysler Avengers to the exotic, oriental Nissan Sunny (from the land of the rising sun: Washington!), he changed them when they had just been run in. But this one was different; he kept his Nissan Almera for years. Money wasn't tight but he never mentioned trading it in for a younger model. His level of mobility was worsening to the point where his right leg was so stiff he couldn't drive.

I researched the options available to help him and found we could replace the old Almera with an automatic car and have it modified to work without foot pedals. It looked like a miracle. He agreed but was uncharacteristically tentative. He was reluctant to let this beaten-up Nissan go. It wasn't anything special - mid-range, small engine, with bumps and scratches on every panel as the bodywork had been used as a primitive parking sensor.

Then the truth came out. "Alice bumped the car just before she died". Even the result of dreadful parking in a supermarket was something to keep his wife close. That bump was part of her. Strangely, he loved it.

We found a buyer who was going to have it as his first car, having recently got married. I told him the story about the bump and he astonished us with his reply. "I'll keep the bump." Dad smiled. Since then, the proud new owner periodically sends photos of him and the car in various coastal locations. He didn't have to start doing that but receiving them certainly puts a smile on my face. Small acts of kindness are remembered forever.

In the meantime, Dad got a beautiful shiny new car modified that he used rarely but it gave him his independence back. "Alice would have loved this car." Result.

Many of us actively use our environment to help us reinforce who we are and remind us of the people who have walked into and out of our lives. Photos, souvenirs and clothing: these foolish things matter.

Even though I was aware that trends in interior design across the nation have taken a turn towards the quirky in recent years, I was confused by what I presumed to be a piece of modern art in an interviewee's living room. I saw a shopping list in the lounge of one of my interviewees - "Weetabix, Frosties, Dairylea, milk". It was framed like a Monet. Why? It was written in their Nan's handwriting. It was the only piece of her handwriting they had found in her house. It made them feel that she was still with them. It was far more powerful than anything I've seen in any gallery before or since.

We should harness these small tokens as comforts. Take control and use this possible venom as a major ingredient in your own anti-venom to heal not hurt. Making a playlist of the songs that make you happy or sad could help. You may find it brings your absent friends closer to you.

On one occasion, I forced myself to listen to 'Superstar' by The Carpenters instead of having to turn over to TalkSport, as I usually would have done. I love the song but it hurt so much. When I could finally get through it, it felt like a mountain had been climbed.

Similarly, the night I was able to sing Andrew Gold's 'Lonely Boy' from start to finish at York Grand Opera House felt like a triumph. I looked up to a seat which had been reserved next to my Dad so he could have extra 'leg room' and smiled. He knew the real reason for that extra seat.

Bob Marley wrote, "When music hits you, you feel no pain". I'm not so sure. Our parents give us the music which stays with us. We grow to love the music they played, even if we hated it at the time just because it wasn't made by whichever Jonny-come-lately artist whose image was

but I doubt they've been the first tracks chosen for final send-offs or couples' first wedded whirls around a dance floor.

Weddings can certainly hurt more than any funeral. My sister's wedding, though a joyous occasion, also hurt. She visited Mam's grave to have a talk at midnight by moonlight the night before. Whilst other brides-to-be would have been enjoying themselves on their second glass of champagne, she was having a cuppa with a teapot and a one-sided prep talk.

papered all over our teenage walls. Nowadays, my Desert Island Discs would pretty much all come from my Mam's record box. Music and magic are but two letters different but often they feel like the same thing. Music is ever-present in happy and sad times, be they major or minor.

When Gerry Goffin and Carole King wrote songs to order to top the charts, they could never have realised the significance those words and melodies would have upon the lives of others. Goffin and King may have written the tracks but as soon as someone else hears them, they become the new and rightful owners forever. Our tunes: not theirs.

The soundtracks to our lives are loaded with emotional connections. First dances, funeral songs, holiday soundtracks... songs mean so much to us. Some may even find some sentimentality in 'Agadoo' or Motorhead's 'The Ace of Spades'

The wedding day in itself is a million-piece jigsaw of planning and execution but if one piece is missing it's hard to take your eyes off it. That night, I slept in my childhood bedroom for the first time in 27 years and let out primal scream after a day surrounded by people all talking about Mam - each turning the screw even tighter - some lovely, some insensitive, some ignorant, some beautiful.

I have found some odd days hurt, too. My birthday hurts. The thought that I am here while the person who did all of the heavy lifting is no longer around to celebrate with me feels deeply unfair.

While more predictable, anniversaries of deaths (or the ANGELVERSARY as Trish Dainton calls the day her husband died), are still hard. Often the lead up to these is worse than the day itself. It can be useful to distract yourself, keep busy or leave it completely free depending on what works for you. In many of these situations, I find children to be the greatest and most effective asset, such is their ability to distract and concentrate on the here and now.

As I once witnessed though, children can sometimes be the triggers themselves. Once, my children went to carol singing in a care home and sang 'Silent Night' to the ladies and gentlemen. After two verses in English, they sang the third in German as they had learnt at school - 'Stille Nacht'. A 96-year-old lady's eyes lit up as she sprang to her feet and started singing whilst holding the children's hands. Tears began to roll down her cheeks.

"My husband was from Austria. He used to sing that to me."

"We're so sorry. We didn't mean to upset you." The children were so apologetic.

"You haven't. These are happy tears. Thank you. That was beautiful."

Once again, some dust got my eye.

Sometimes we don't even need outside stimuli to set us off. As one interviewee said, "I don't need photos or old VHS cassettes with their tabs removed. I have every laugh, every smile, and every image when I close my eyes." Of course, problems arise if you find you can't do this as easily any more and that's when video and photos can be invaluable. The trouble is that the leading

man you are looking for may have always been behind the camera. Just like Hollywood, home videos seem to have a disproportionate number of male directors. Ensure that the men of the family don't insist on being Spielberg all of the time because when it comes to having videos of him he'll be shouting "Cut" when you want to see him in "Action".

These foolish things may not be so foolish. Perhaps they more closely resemble 'raindrops on roses and whiskers on kittens, bright copper kettles and warm woollen mittens. These foolish things may be a few of your favourite things. If they can help… keep them close to you.

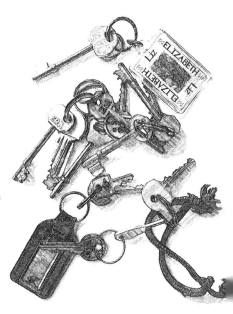

Don't You Forget About Me

In memory of
Roger Bucklesby.
Who hated this park.
and everyone in it.

"I'd love for my life to be commemorated with a small plaque on an uncomfortable bed for tramps, to have cheap, two-litre bottles of electric white cider quaffed by urban alcoholics, and occasionally to be urinated on by dogs..." said no one, ever. Yet many a park bench has a plaque with a cradle-to-grave billing. I always look at the "1906-1972" and wonder what they did in the dash in-between.

My mother-in-law can't walk past a park bench without reading its brass engraving; it can feel like driving with the brakes on if you are in a hurry. The finest we saw, in New York's Central Park, made her chuckle. It said: "I've always bloody hated this park and everyone who uses it."

The best tributes keep the memory alive; they have the person living on in some way, keeping them close to us. If people are still being spoken about, do they ever truly die?

On the CBBC website, I saw an amazing and moving video clip.

"Where's Mummy?" asked Dad, after a bedtime story.

"In our hearts."

Possibly the best answer I have ever heard. At that point, a speck of dust may have got in my eye.

A tribute doesn't have to be an obelisk of the finest marble; it can be a seed grown in the garden that, in years to come, will give you apples.

Every time my friend, Ian, hits a snare or crashes a cymbal, it's because his Dad planted that love of music deep within him, chauffeuring him and his kit to every gig. He even used his car-spraying skills to give him the most breath-taking bespoke kit. Every band he plays in is a tribute band - to his late Dad.

In Papua New Guinea, women have fingers and ears amputated to show how much they miss their men. Thankfully, they are given an anaesthetic in the form of a punch on the arm. Strangely the men don't bother, having decided that the fairer sex's piano playing should suffer. How can this be right in modern times?

Fran, having researched her grandmother's life while preparing her eulogy, decided to write up Grandma's life story as a children's book. She had her sister illustrate it, then had copies printed for grandkids, great-grandkids and future generations, like a pop-up version of Who Do You Think You Are?

My mother has a standard headstone, two graves away from a gravestone designed as a pint of Guinness. I can't help thinking she'd smile about that. When wondering how to commemorate her, my Dad came up with the idea of raising money to transform an unused piece of wasteland next to the primary school where she had been head governor, creating a beautiful, secret garden with a hand-crafted, story-telling seat, engraved with a poem.

On Mam's birthday and wedding anniversaries, Dad picks up his stick and slowly wanders down for a chat. It's a special place and the words sum up everything that mattered to her. As head governor, she was involved in the everyday running of the school. She didn't want to be called Mrs. Donaghy, but the headteacher didn't feel it appropriate to be too informal calling her Alice; a compromise was reached with "Mrs. Alice", so the hand-carved story-telling 'throne' reads:

Mrs Alice
A hundred years from now,
It will not matter
What my bank account was,
The sort of house I lived in,
Or the kind of car I drove,
But the world may be different
Because I was important
In the life of a child.

My Dad's parents were buried next to one another, 20 years apart. He has never returned to the graves, although they are only a mile from his armchair. "There's nothing there for me there. It's just grass. My memories are with me, even after all these years."

Tommy Whitelaw has transformed the thinking about dementia care in Scotland, following caring for his mother. This legacy will make a difference for everyone else in similar situations, decades from now.

Zoe Harris's husband had dementia. Staff in the care home he was living in were getting so much wrong with his care, making assumptions without asking. She could have turned on the staff, but instead, she saw a greater need affecting thousands in a similar situation - so she created Care Charts, making things easier for staff to grasp what matters. These charts were a simple pictorial record, a fitting tribute, that have given her a raison d'etre, a focus that makes a difference while raising a glass to her late husband.

So, people did not die in vain. We can't get them back, but can we learn from a mistake? Ensure that others don't have to endure this? If mistakes happen once, they may be forgiven, but if they happen again and again, it shows that nobody cares.

Bruce Wayne created Batman to make sure nobody would go through losing his parents as he did.

Where tattoos once acted as war paint, now they're often used to make peace and to keep someone close. Whereas some people have ink done out of boredom, others need a constant reminder as a part of them.

One interviewee lost the love of his life and the mother of his three children in her fifties. Since then, he has become a canvas paying tribute to his wife; tattoos tell their story, screaming out to everyone he meets that he wants to be asked what these inked enigmas signify, to start the conversation he needs to have. They act as multi-coloured ice-breakers, sharing stories and keeping her alive by his side.

Unlike most regulars to tattoo studios, Richard was desperate for them to hurt - but they didn't. That lack of pain really hurt! But they stand proudly, a gallery over his arms. Never will you see his sleeves rolled down. He is proud of who she was, what she meant to him and his children, and how much she still does.

Gordon Train has his Dad's nickname "Choo Choo" tattooed on to his fingers in a way one set upside down the other the correct way up so that when he sings and plays his guitar, his Dad's name can be seen to all audience members as the man who supported his love of music.

Tattoos can even be made from the ashes of a dead relative. I can't help thinking many wouldn't fancy that, but these are all about what works for you.

"I love it when someone avoids the bog-standard designs on the wall and asks for something bespoke that is personal and important to them. I always put more into those tattoos, seeing people cry with tears of joy as they leave the chair, knowing their lost loved one will always be near."

Ellie Holmes comes from a big family whose grandmother was the loud heart and soul of the family. She never shied away from a party so, when she died, the family decided to give her a send-off worthy of the life she'd led. Whereas some lives are like a candle flickering in the corner, their Nan's was a display of pyrotechnics. So, they approached a firework company to put her ashes into a large rocket. They sent her up into the sky, off with one last bang, as she illuminated them for a final time.

"This may shock some, but it summed her up perfectly. The tribute has to fit the person, no matter how outrageous it may appear to detached spectators. Their opinion means nothing."

Sometimes, we don't have the words to express how we feel, so we hide away and express our feelings in creative ways, helping us to grieve.

One man, following the death of his youngest daughter and wife, turned his life around with a lathe, creating bespoke furniture and fruit bowls, hiding away from the world in a shed. No awkward questions to answer, just a man and his tools. He spent his days removing sharp edges to make them perfectly smooth and ready to take pride of place in other people's homes.

One interviewee's Dad died and left him enough money to buy a car. Many would have done just that but, instead, the TV sports cameraman bought a rough woodland, a place to escape the pressures of everyday life and become at one with the trees. Planting, chopping, sawing, pruning… he created Little Land, a haven for his family and friends. So much more than a Mondeo estate whose value would dwindled and been much less therapeutic.

Some have taken old military uniforms and shirts to make other clothes for children, or to make pillowcases, duvets, teddies - a subtle way of keeping that person close to you forever.

I saw one instance where a bride's mother had recently died, so she used pieces of her mum's wedding dress to make details on hers. These little things can be the biggest difference and make you feel they are with you.

One interviewee always carries something pink in her bag for her daughter who died - despite her never liking the colour previously. My sister, Anna, wears our mother's engagement ring; it startles me every time I look without being prepared. It's moving as she has similar hands. After the initial shock, I smile, because it's so much better than the ring being buried underground. I can't help thinking Mam would be very proud of the hand where it lives today.

Whether it's a sponsored walk, a golf tournament or a bungee jump, the things we do as a tribute either to raise money, raise awareness, raise a smile or raise a glass can all be the "perfect" tribute.

If we lose someone, often the most empowering thing is to create something new. Setting up a charity can be good for the family, but also for all those who benefit. Whether it is Gloria Hunniford, Jane Tomlinson or Ronan Keating, their labours of love have impacted on thousands of lives. The Bobby Robson Foundation has given many more 90 minutes extra time to thousands of people. Tim Lloyd Yeates' momentum made sure his inspirational Alive Activities for older people continues long after he left us far too early.

In 2013, Jo Cole became a widow aged 39 when her husband, Neil, died suddenly; her son was eight years old. She found it difficult to find support for him, so decided something special needed to be done. After tirelessly trawling the internet and filling in forms, she set up a much-needed charity for the area's bereaved families - "Bereaved Children Support York".

"I was surprised there wasn't really anything available in a large city like York for children who had experienced the death of someone close to them. I was determined that no other families would feel so isolated."

I can't help thinking my friend, Neil, would be astonished at the tenacity of his wife.

Whether it's happy memory ribbons, making things for Daddy or grandchildren doing a project about their dead grandparents, activities like this can be useful for all. What good are dusty photos in a drawer? iPads can now be filled with photographs, playlists of favourite songs, videos and lives creating

a wonderful, historic resource for generations past, present and future.

Many stunning, beautiful songs have been written after close friends or relatives have died. "Tears in Heaven" by Eric Clapton, "Empty Garden" by Elton John, "Jesus to a Child" by George Michael - all exquisite songs, but many others have been written by unknown musicians and they matter just as much.

Writing and recording dreadful songs that all sound the same, that rhyme as badly as "pneumonia" and "phone ya". These aren't to be assessed as pieces of art by critics; Germaine Greer won't feature them on the Late Review. The process is far more important than the result, just like kids' artwork on a fridge door; it's all beautiful to you, no matter how dreadful in reality. Remember, nobody ever erected a statue for a critic, but perhaps a few have had a park bench dedicated to them.

I have seen care staff lining hospital corridors, making a human archway for those they felt honoured to have cared for. I've seen an army of mourners in black suits form a human snowplough to clear a backstreet, so a man could get to his wife's funeral where the hearse could not have reached. This showed the love for both him and his wife.

It can be a little idea... following the loss of his mother, Ian and his brother decided to make a weekly pilgrimage to the pub quiz with their Dad. It worked a treat and eventually bore fruit, so much so they often suffered sneering, dirty looks from their competitors as they entered the pub - the highest praise any pub quiz team can receive from their peers! Two years on, his father became too ill to attend the quiz and he eventually died. Even now, the brothers still go - because their Dad would like it, and so do they. Simple. Effective. A wonderful, ongoing tribute.

The Wilsons staged a memorial concert for their father, six months after they lost him. It was a stunning evening of ego-free performances, raising more than £4,000 in a sweatbox venue, but the true success was that it provided a focus for the family and fused their community, creating an event where their Dad would have loved a front row seat.

One man was so tight, the buffet at his funeral had prices on every item and a till at the end to highlight his frugal nature. "Like Tommy would ever pay for everyone's tea! If a bill came to £1 between three of them, he'd insist someone else paid the 34p!"

If you died tomorrow, who'd miss you? What would your end-of-term report read like? What mess would you leave behind? What legacy?

Perhaps the greatest tribute is US. How many of us look in the mirror and see our mother's eyes, our father's smile or our grandfather's receding hairline? We're made of bits of people we no longer have. We may be the true tribute - an on-going champion of their values, vision and passion, so long as those values also matter to us. It would be an ill-fitting tribute, to do something that you didn't believe in; absent friends wouldn't thank us for hypocrisy.

I'd never have recognised the person I am today before losing my mother. Root to branch, I've changed. Things that mattered before, now don't; all goalposts have changed. Doing good is so much better than doing well nowadays. Success is measured in words and deeds, not pounds and pence. I wish it hadn't taken losing her to create this new me. How sad it is that it takes something as drastic as someone dying to remind us how to live; that "happy" really is the new "rich", and that money is worthless when compared to time.

I stood on the stage at York Grand Opera House and sang one of my Mam's favourite songs - "Lonely Boy" - a year after being unable to. I looked up at the empty seat I kept so my Dad had more leg room, (he knew, as did I, why the seat was really reserved), and smiled. Sometimes, doing something that hurts, and getting through it, feels amazing.

Perhaps you only truly die when people forget you? If it makes them feel close to you, as if they haven't really gone, that's a tribute worthy of the best.

The Age of Innocence

Children are honest- straight talking - they don't do euphemism - they do route one . They don't want to know that Granddad has 'gone to sleep' or the rabbit has 'run off to play with his friends.'

If they want an answer they will ask a question. Then if it isn't the answer they want they ask another question and will use "Why?" with the tenacity of an expert interrogator.

There is no escape. They are rarely fobbed off as easily as adults.

Paxman would look on and wince.

Children see things differently. Adults go through life feeling like they are a burden. Children never do. Someone must have that wrong then...

1 in 29 children lose a parent or sibling in their school career. That's one per class and yet education fails these children too busy covering more 'vital' topics on the curriculum to give an A,B,C or D answer to with a HB pencil line between the two dots!

Virtually every school's website boasts catchy soundbites that they prepare children for the life ahead yet few back this up.

Imagine if one came clean "we teach kids how to jump through hoops to pass exams" or "we'll tick the boxes to get them to university so they can tick similar boxes but with linger essays".

Many avoid tackling the most difficult challenges in life that could prove essential in years to come . Instead schools focus on league tables. School reputation in tact until next August!

Hitting the target. Missing the point.

I can write an A grade essay about Bismarck and the Franco-Prussian War, tell you everything you'd ever want to know about an amoeba and solve any quadratic equation you wish to throw at me but nothing was ever mentioned about the impact of someone dying. It would also have been useful to have a lesson on how to change a tyre and win the odd argument when you are obviously in the wrong!

These goalposts change instantly when a student dies within a school. Suddenly necessity becomes the mother of invention as innovative ideas are used to support all parties.

Priorities are turned on their heads as everyone realises life can't and doesn't just go on -it is too important to be ignored as teachers, students and all school community grieve. Data laden spreadsheets are quickly forgotten as all computers are put on standby.

Surely we should be less reactive. We need to pre-empt and educate giving young people the insight, skills and greater understanding. Life is a trapeze act. We need to have the safety net there to catch them before they fall.

We should learn from children and watch how they interact with one another. Their minds aren't yet made up. They are better , more natural uninhibited communicators than us. They don't see the carpet of eggshells that 'grown ups' tiptoe across. At what point did we forget how to talk to one another?

When one young mother died leaving two young sons under-five the other children were there at break-time playing and including the brothers - without a hint of isolation or fear.

The school gate mafia quickly followed suit. Mums gathered like cow elephants collectively maternal-subconsciously making a little bit more love each, cheering a little louder at assemblies and providing extra applause on sports day where a visiting Nana stood in place of her daughter. I called it 'auto-parent' the beautiful innate default setting factory-fitted in mothers.

They realised that it could easily have been them. It was as if each parent had bought shares in seeing these boys make their mother proud. A beautiful thing that shows what we can do when we see a need.

When one little boy died in a school after a long illness parents came together for the funeral. Coffins shouldn't have to come in such small sizes. Superheroes are for lunch boxes and pyjamas not coffins.

All of the mums clung onto the only Dad able to take the afternoon off-empathetic to a woman at the front for whom their imagination could not stretch.Then when a long-serving popular teacher fell ill then died the school rallied round again. One school had to learn many lessons . The Headteacher was an amazing lady who supported everyone.

"You've got me. Who's got you?" was a line Lois Lane once said to Superman. I felt the same seeing her every day. None of this was covered in her PGCE. There were no boxes for these challenges in her lesson plans.

Sheena Powley, a marvellous lady whose well chosen words will resonate and equip these young people in years to come. When she retired from the school she left with the respect of everyone for her invaluable care for all of her school community.

Elsewhere Jo, a mother widowed at 38 asked questions

"Is Johnny doing this because he's lost his Dad or because he's 9?"

She had no experience of either. Kids need help from parents but parents struggle too… both may be made of bits of the person they've lost. Perhaps we should listen more to the brightest members of our families whose wisdom lies in their innocence, inexperience and honesty.

At what stage did we start thinking we, the grown-ups, the self-proclaimed decision-makers are the ones with all of the answers?

Holding Back The Years

When people die, many people "filter" their faults, leaving a distilled, refined version - even Oliver Cromwells can become poster boys over time. When speaking to people for this book, something else happened... I asked people two questions: "How old was the person you lost when they died?" and "How old are they when you see them in your mind?"

Very few think of Paul Newman as an 83 year old, or Patrick Swayze as a man, gaunt, in his final rounds with cancer. Each of them has a place in time and our hearts, though... many remember Newman's steely blue eyes as a young man, or Johnny Castle lifting Baby in Dirty Dancing. It's often similar with our absent friends.

Some people have harsh images, engraved in their memories, of people dying, unable to soften their focus and fade them away to replace with happier times. Many others see their loved ones as much younger.

"Dad is always in his late thirties, tanned and at his best when he appears in dreams - but he died at 76".

Many benefit from turning back the clock, way beyond any TV makeover, to times with smaller waists, long before they had a good knee and a bad one!

"My dad lost his leg through contracting MRSA during a kidney transplant when he was 75 - in my dreams, he always has both legs!"

My mother is forty, the same age she is in a picture at the bottom of our stairs, just before having my sister and twenty two years before she died. For me, she will always be that age. I love that I have managed to rip out the pages where she was dying.

Some, who have lost siblings and friends as children, strangely imagine them at the age they would be today, even forty years on, using other siblings or parents as points of reference for how they might appear now. Is this uncommon?

One thing is certain: the pecking order in a family never changes, no matter who dies. If you were the middle child, that's who you are, even if the older or younger child has died. It seems that pecking order is factory-fitted, ingrained and permanent. No middle child's chip on the shoulder miraculously disappeared from all those interviewed. One lady, who had an older sister die at forty five, said "Even though its five years ago, I can't imagine her younger than me, so I imagine her as if she's still alive, always three years older than me; my big sister".

Others remember siblings as small children, even if they died in their 20s or 30s, possibly in a simpler, happier, carefree time.

These are the virtual versions that we keep with us, they're who we see when we close our eyes and who visit us in dreams. At whatever age, if these versions can help us feel closer to them, we should be thankful.

Hurt

"No pain no gain".

Perhaps that's true…

If you could have any super power what would it be? The ability to fly? Invisibility? Super strength or be able to shoot stuff out of your hands like virtually every Marvel comic hero? No… I'd choose time travel every time. That one power would end all hurt in an instant.

Pain and heartbreak would be things of the past as you could always rewind to happier times. Perhaps that's why films and TV are obsessed with it. If DeLoreans could really do something special at 88mph they would outsell all other vehicles. People wouldn't say WHERE they were going on holiday but WHEN.

Nobody would lose anybody. We could walk back through locked doors and never forget anything as we could revisit points in time instantly with all senses alive reliving our favourite groundhog days. Feelings recaptured at will…

Unfortunately pain is many people's daily bread but is there a strange comfort in discomfort?

"I hurt myself today

To see if I could feel." (Hurt by Nine Inch Nails)

If I am happy, have I in some way betrayed the person I have lost? I should be hurt not happy.

Anaesthetists make it their life's work to protect us from physical pain. Few embark on root canal treatment without an injection to make their bottom lip feel like rubber. But many of us want to feel a sense of loss. Is there pleasure in pain? Not sadomasochism but a strangely rewarding feeling of grasping the nettle; doing things that we know will make us cry and show us how much someone really mattered. Are our tears a direct correlation to how much we loved them? If I don't cry did they not matter?

How many holiday readers love a good cry through their sun cream onto their waterproof Kindles? Cinemas and television feed on this hurt-lust with Beaches, The Champ and My Girl having audiences sobbing. Disney -the home of hurt and heartbreak- is as guilty as anyone, from Bambi's mother dying to Finding Nemo, which could have been called Losing Mum. Even Elsa and Ana

were orphaned long before everyone has a singalong of 'Let It Go'. The list is endless…

Having recently lost my children's Grandma, I saw a trailer for a film called UP about a grumpy old white-haired man with a house covered in balloons. It seemed a perfectly harmless escape in the darkness with a bucket of popcorn for the kids on such an upsetting day, only to find the film was actually about a recently widowed man (who was the spitting image of their Granddad) who adored his wife and was battling a life of loneliness. No warning was given by our friends at Pixar!

Yet so many people like to cry in the darkness and be the last person to leave at the end with puffy eyes. It's a release. Death wins Oscars. Grief scoops up BAFTAs. Songs in minor keys are almost always the songs that make it onto mix tapes connecting fledgling romances. Barry Manilow famously sang, "I write the songs that make the young girls cry." - Despite not actually writing it.

So are hurt, heartbreak and pain sources of our entertainment? Like venturing onto rollercoasters to heighten certain emotions, do we enjoy these upsetting voyeuristic journeys into the upset of others to retrace our own painful footsteps like a virtual empathy ride?

Very few soldiers returning home want to have their battle scars removed. Many war veterans kept their shrapnel in situ as souvenirs of survival. We often like to compare wounds - not for point scoring but to explain how they got there.

Hurt can also be born from regret. In our final hours, if we were shown the pie chart of how much time we have spent with people who neither care nor matter in our lives compared to the ones around our bed- how proud would we be?

Have work commitments and insignificant others stopped you from spending valuable time and doing things with those who really matter? Sometimes we try so hard to earn a living we forget how to live. This can be even worse if it has stopped us seeing someone before the end of their lives. Sometimes we live life like we're going to get another one. There is no "Insert 50p to Continue" in life's arcade game. James Bond will not return in "Octopussy" and Batman will not be back same Bat time, same Bat channel! How often does work enjoy the best of us as family are left with what's left: the weak-end?

How many are haunted by the last words being in raised voices in an argument? One interviewee had this revisit him with panic attacks even twenty years later. We must somehow tear out this last page of their autobiography and realise that this was a tiny fraction of their lives. Instead, remember that you enjoyed an overwhelming aggregate win.

Kate Bush wrote, "If I only could I'd make a deal with God and get him to swap our places. I'd be running up that road, running up that hill with no problem." They died. You didn't. It's the people left behind with the survivor's guilt. It is a medal rarely worn with pride for the passenger who escaped the car crash where their friends didn't but it was not their fault. You have no reason to seek forgiveness.

Whether consciously or not, some revisit the pain and dwell regularly in replaying the tape. One interviewee told me, "I have a recurring dream not of a 19 year old but of a little girl aged 7 or 8, unkempt, who I try to help. I stretch out to hold her but I can't quite reach. It feels so vivid."

Following the loss of a child, some of my interviewees considered this question: "Should I go with her and you stay behind?" Is this so irrational? When a child dies, parents struggle. 70% of marriages end in divorce following the loss of a child because both parties have lost very different relationships as mothers and fathers. They follow totally different paths at different speeds often in different directions. Some seek counselling. Some fight on alone. Some want to hide. Some yearn to be surrounded by people. Some are so different but hope that they have one thing in common- needing each other and therefore they end up taking turns to lean on the other.

Sometimes, we want to feel our own personal pain in cathartic commemoration. One interviewee, widowed in his early 50s, said, "I wanted tattoos to show every aspect of life with my wife. I wanted them to hurt. Sadly they didn't."

Doctors generously offer of schmorgasbord of tranquilisers, anti-depressants and sleeping tablets. Many don't want to be mogadonned from this; they want to feel the pain. Numbness feels detached. Some need to fight their own battles. Some don't want to heal. They want to be able to tap into it and enjoy it on their terms. As I write this I know the word enjoy will jar but I believe for many it is the right word. Hurt can help... if we can harness this energy we can eventually turn it into something positive.

One grandmother who had both husband and daughter die said, "I've had my happiness. I'm biding time - my long life is punishment for surviving them-treading water hoping to drown." Sad but meant...

"I often cry myself asleep. I've even cried myself awake before!" Some of us like a good cry- it is a release - a reboot - it shows we are alive - hurting shows we feel. Perhaps photograph album cellophane wasn't to protect from grubby fingerprints but from our tears. Crying helps lift the ships from harbour. Many love the smell after the rain: petrichor (I didn't even realise it had a name but Google did). And following the rain we get rainbows.

However, while everybody hurts, the same cannot be said of crying. Some can't cry. From the outside, they seem to have no release with their arid eyes. Others look on thinking they don't feel the pain but it may be even worse. No pain. No gain?

While some are determined to move on following loss; "when my wife died of cancer, I wasn't going to let there be any more casualties," for some, the hurt can simply be too much. As Debbie Reynolds and Carrie Fisher reminded us, some don't live long after losing someone close. One lady, after losing her husband following years of Lewy Body Dementia, was left lost. She died six days later. The doctor couldn't write "of a broken heart" on her death certificate but her work was done. As a lady with a strong faith, she wanted to be by his side.

Whether 'good grief' (for some, an oxymoron) or bad, it does hurt. Memories hurt. People don't want to forget - they want to remember and hurt may be the price we pay for these memories. It's worth remembering that the brightest light casts the longest shadows. The Tin Man asked a man behind a curtain for a heart, even though his life would have been so much easier as he was. He would avoided heartbreak but missed out on so much more. If I could make you bulletproof-emotionless, like a machine- how many would take me up on the offer? If I could remove the memories that aren't wrapped in a red ribbon but the ones in a black tin buried away, how many would say YES? We are a stockpot of everything good and bad that has happened to us: the joy and the hurt. As Rainer Maria Riike wrote "Please don't take my devils away for my angels may flee too".

You Make Me Feel Brand New

"Dad, may I borrow your pen?"

"Yes, but I'll need it back. It's my special pen. My Parker. It lives in my top pocket all the time. Your Mam got it me for Christmas back in the '70s. It's had more refills than I can remember, ruined two good shirts and I've super-glued that clip that falls off three times - so it's good as the day I got it. If you pull down the lid of the bureau, you'll see I've even got the box it came in!"

Dad clearly took pride that he had still had its plastic container.

Just as some people feel naked without their watch or wedding ring, Dad felt the same way not having his special Parker pen in his pocket, next to his heart. Whenever something important needed signing, out it came: cheques, letter of resignation, will, death certificate... Even Christmas cards that he had never, ever written before being widowed. That pen was his constant companion in a world of variables, exits and disappointments. It mattered to him. It was like an old friend - a gift given with love and he loved it back.

Relationships are often disposable - even though we hope they may be more permanent. Rarely do things feel as special as my Dad's Parker pen.

Look after your friends. Know where they are and what they need to help them feel their best. It may take up your time and effort, but it's better to have a wonderful Parker pen next to your heart than a big pile of disposable biros in your bin.

Father Figure

"My Dad's doing my head in"

"I'm sick of him telling me what to do! Who does he think he is?"

Two throwaway comments in the sixth form common room made my blood boil. I made a hasty exit for a cig. They were complaining about a luxury I'd kill for.

They had their Dads-even if estranged or divorced they could visit them, speak on the phone or even just receive a text. They had a choice and chose not to bother.

I was the man of the house... at twelve. Some job adverts read "no training necessary". This was no training at all!

I was drawing the map as I bounded through and most days I got lost. I'd snarl at men trying to curry favour with my Mum-like sabotaging a potential house sale by messing up the rooms, not flushing the toilets, cooking kippers or commenting on how vile the neighbours are.

It was my job to ensure these Prince Charmings' glass slippers were shattered long before reaching her feet. Nobody could replace Dad.

She was far too good for them. They didn't come close. She didn't need them anyway-she had me. She was MINE not theirs. I'd already lost my Dad I sure as hell wasn't going to let a total stranger take Mum as well.

I was so protective. Looking back perhaps a little over-protective.

Bizarrely, I was being taught how to be a man by women!

It's pretty hard to ask your Mam 'Dad questions' about how odd women are! So I asked Dad for advice in quiet moments hoping he'd answer. Like saying prayers to someone not so almighty but much more important.

I didn't know where to find peace. None of my friends 'got me' anymore. One day I had everything in common with them the next - nothing! It was like arriving from another planet-I looked like them but knew my life was alien to them so I sought refuge elsewhere and got lost in books, poetry and words. Fiction made more sense as Fact had let me down writing my favourite character out far too early in the novel.

A city adopted me far enough over the Scottish border to be away but near enough to be home in an hour if Mum needed me.

I needed a job to pay my way through uni and fill my hours. Enter stage left a foul-mouthed Glaswegian landlord with a pint of lager where others had a right hand. Nobody significant-just my new boss. I never realised just how important he would become .I never saw it initially but he adopted me, saw what I needed, looked after me, gave an eye to me, ripped the p#ss out of me . He was a Dad with kids of his own who lived abroad. Perhaps we were sent to help each other.

I don't know if he knew. I think he must have.

Over the years my 2:1 in English Literature was used to pull pints and change barrels talking to strangers as I served them one too many. I listened. I learnt. Hoping to find wisdom amongst the barflies' drunken ramblings.

Then one day, much later than advertised, and predicted I felt confident enough to leave this comfort zone and finally fly away able to stand alone ready for a new life, a new career as someone's husband.

I still ask Dad for advice in quiet moments. I invited him to the wedding. I hope he came but I never saw him.

I wish I had been given the chance to be a kid like my friends-to grow up before I became the man of the house. I may not have been so aggressive or made so many mistakes. Mam put us first and her second. She always has.

She's still by herself. My biggest regret was scaring those men away. I know now that was selfish. Perhaps one of those men I set packing could have been the one to make her smile.

She deserves to be happy. We all do.

A Family Affair

"You can't choose your family."

Throughout this book there are stories where family members have exceeded all expectation to become the key catalyst in helping people survive losing someone close to them but birds of a feather don't always flock together; sometimes it can be more like a dogfight.

We hope we should have more in common than eye colour, pattern baldness or bunions. We expect to be as close as the Waltons where if you kick one they all limp but having people die can turn families into the most vile, undignified game of Hungry Hippos known to man where medals for bravery are put on Ebay long before anyone notices they are gone. It may be worth remembering that Happy Families is a game where you compete to have more cards than your competitors...

Although the saying goes, "Blood is thicker than water", it's worth remembering that it's also far more poisonous! This is perhaps where families get it wrong. They think it's about BLOOD not LOVE... about WHO they are and not HOW they are with one another! There may be a Cain and Abel on every street.

How many wedding guests are invited out of obligation because they have the same surname and not because they matter? People who you've only seen over the years in that same suit again whether staring into a font, picking confetti out of their hair or wiping away tears. Often we turn to friends instead - people we chose to like and don't have to pretend to like- the family we choose - whose noses aren't necessarily as near to the painting as ours so they can give a more objective, balanced view.

Sometimes, that objective view tells us that our similarities can divide us more than our differences. One problem many families encounter is when a son follows in his father's footsteps so much that they clash. When apples don't fall far from the tree-identical jigsaw pieces rarely tessellate! Not everyone has parents they can look up to. As one interviewee admitted, "The one gift my Dad showed me was how NOT to be a father!" .Some parents are more suited to Jeremy Kyle than Little House on the Prairie.

It seems bizarre that dog walkers will strike up a conversation when they have just one thing in common yet some siblings won't speak despite previously sharing so much. Many don't talk in order to avoid opening wounds and hurting the other. This can lead to a stalemate where nobody gets upset but nothing will ever change.

Many families have self-elected figureheads who talk a good fight always telling people what should happen and how they know best yet are never willing to back up this rhetoric with actions. As one interviewee commented, "I have an enormous family yet when my brother died I could only see my footprints in the sand. The rest buried their heads in it", proving that in families, small doesn't necessarily mean close knit and big isn't always better!

Sometimes families can be closed shops as unwilling to welcome outsiders as the villagers in Deliverance. Michelle was made to feel unwelcome at her own husband's funeral in Ireland. It was clear to all-comers this was their funeral for their son and their brother not for some 'late to the party' wife. "His family took over. I was superseded , surplus to requirements, washed over, palmed off. God got a better seat than me. I'd not noticed God visit before."

Often when the father of a family dies there is a realisation that the one thing they had in common has gone. The anchor that held them in harbour; the hub of the wheel has gone and now the spokes (with nothing in common) are turning on one another-the once perfect circle of brothers and sisters now buckled forever. They are strangers who once shared hand me down clothes, DNA and a postcode but are now just middle-aged women comparing children's achievements and sending equally-priced Christmas presents who now happen to have a share in an ex-council house in Wigan.

"Dad was the man with the answers even if we didn't ask for them or want to hear them. The man who'd always tell you so without ever saying 'I told you so'. The man who told you 'you're far too good for that waster!' as I thought Prince Charming -the one-had left me.

After losing Dad we suddenly realised none of us had ever made an important decision in our lives.

Everything went through him and he always had a one man veto. Dad knew best. He was the head and heart of the family; remove the Sun and we become icy blocks of stone orbiting nothing. Monthly text messages and politeness at best but never will we huddle around the warm hearth that was Dad."

It can be even worse. For some, monthly texts and politeness would be a comparative ideal. One lady recounted how her five sisters turned on one another bickering over money and jewellery following their father dying. "This would have disgusted and destroyed Dad." If her father had just written on a piece of paper "Never turn against one another "I think his wishes would have been respected. The problem is people always seem to intend to write things like that 'tomorrow'... when that tomorrow doesn't happen, the real mess begins.

Not all mothers would take a bullet for their babies. In one instance, a wife doted on her husband as she felt he would be there long after her children would 'leave her' (as she put it.) She put loyalty to her husband (whether right or wrong) ahead of her children. She always sided with him. As some are referred to as God-fearing she was perhaps husband-fearing. No relationship should have fear on its list of ingredients.

Whilst hiding in her husband's shadow she left her son orphaned by silence. Mother and son stopped talking when the Beatles were still

recording, with neither of them ever considering a truce... for 41 years. They saw each other across the city centre square but never once acknowledged the other or spoke despite each of them being the other's only living blood relative.

Everyone assumed Jack's mother had died years ago. He had no reason to say otherwise so friends adopted him. They became his family who would always be there for him as he'd be there for them. He found out about his mother's death from a two inch square announcement in the obituaries column. He had planned to boycott her funeral but reluctantly attended after an eleventh hour change of heart wearing dirty overalls and steelies he stood silently at the back of a sparsely populated church. Last in. First out. Nothing said.

When asked why he and his Mother stopped speaking in 1969 he shared the heart-breaking answer... "I can't remember." One apology- even if it wasn't sincere could have prevented 41 years of silent stubbornness. Nobody won. It wasn't a draw. They both lost 41 - 0.

It seems strange that without a will everything automatically goes to people who may not care or be aware if you were dead or alive just because they have the same bloodline. One executor for a will noticed previously invisible relatives crawl out from the woodwork - people who had never been seen before... circling like vultures, never sent a birthday card nor visited but because of being 'twice removed' (whatever that means) they thought they had won the lottery without a ticket as the heirless widow died.

Hypocrisy was the key feature in every conversation as they spoke warmly of a lady they had only known by the name of her and her dog in Christmas cards with enclosed Woolworths vouchers. They clambered around offering to redecorate her house out of the goodness of their hearts... painting with clammy hands whilst vulgar car brochures covered the coffee table awaiting the three bars to line up and the jackpot to rattle onto the floor but it came out lemons...

No big windfall came-instead the local animal shelter was funded for years, a memorial rugby tournament would live on for decades and her and her husband's graves would be tended for 40 years whilst her neighbours who were always on hand were left thank you cheques to pay for a holiday each. The unknown space invaders who came expecting golden eggs were left with a Kinder surprise.

Family is everything... but not every family fit the idylls found on a cornflake box. Sometimes families fall short.

Don't blame yourself. After all, you didn't choose them!

122

We Don't Talk Anymore

The summer of '79 saw Cliff Richard's "We don't talk anymore" knock The Boomtown Rats "I don't like Mondays" off the No.1 slot. Little did I know how prophetic this would be…

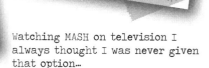

From as early as I could remember, Mum had always loved me and made me feel safe - but deep down, we knew she lived under a cloud that she could never shake off.

I was sixteen. Death happened to old people… and other people. We used to say "Cross my heart and hope to die…" but they were just words, learnt parrot fashion. I never thought anyone would expect us to see it through. My Mum was forty two when she left.

I couldn't go into school, armed with tales of illness to open sympathetic floodgates, because Mum's death certificate had the word "Suicide" on it.

"Suicide is painless

It brings on many changes

And I can take or leave it if I please…"

Watching MASH on television I always thought I was never given that option…

Some lives end with a full stop. Some end with an exclamation mark. Mum's ended with a question mark.

Mum left us. She wasn't taken from us. She went without saying goodbye. When she took her life, she took a lot of mine too. So much of me died that day, without any explanation. I was left with one sentence, though, whirring around in my head: "I'll show you".

Over the years, this has burned in my heart whenever I'm told I can't do something. I can't tell you how much I've needed to cling onto those words for nearly forty years! Forty years with no phone calls, no words of encouragement, no sharing of experiences. Nothing!

Mum was poorly - "bi-polar" was unheard of in the days of Starsky and Hutch - and no-one was there for her, or able to help. Those were the days of "fight your own battles" and "pull yourself together, woman!"

Taking her own life was perhaps her way of protecting us from what she was living through - and what might lie ahead. She must have been desperate.

Someone once said to me that bad things often happen to good people, and that I wasn't a bad person who deserved such a harsh punishment. I can't tell you how desperately I hung onto to those words.

I have a few photos of Mum, but precious few objects. Nothing really illustrates my memories, as she was so much more than just a collection of trinkets. My memories have been kind to me, leaving me the things I choose to remember, filtering the darkness and leaving only the lighter, happier times. In that way, time may be a healer.

I spoke to whoever would listen, whoever could help to soften the blow at that point in my life. I soon learnt that guilt helps no-one. Blame helps even fewer.

Forgiving yourself is the hardest forgiveness to find, especially if you are not even sure what it is you've done - if anything.

It haunts me that the last time Mum hugged me I was too busy, wrapped up in my teenage world, to hug her back. I wish I could turn back time, to remedy this one detail. "Sorry" doesn't seem to cover it, even after all these years. It's my biggest regret.

The years give perspective, allowing me to enjoy her at her beautiful best. I can see now that it wasn't my fault, but many years passed before I could see this through the tears.

She never saw me studying. She never opened my exam results. She never saw me go to university. She never met my first boyfriend - who she'd have hated! She never saw me pass my driving test. She never saw me buy my first car. She never saw me become a Mum with a successful career...

But I hope I've made her proud.

That little 16 year old girl, crying over her records, could never have dreamt of being the woman I am today.

I guess I showed you...

Ashes To Ashes

At one point, cavemen must have noticed one of their number hadn't picked up his club for some time so they had to decide if they would burn, bury or eat him. Thankfully, time and civilisation has whittled away one of the options but how far have we really evolved?

Who is a funeral really for? Is it for show in the way some weddings are planned to trump their friends - surely funerals don't fall into this mire of bridezilla point-scoring? We still spend money on a party without the guest of honour being present. Like an overpriced, belated birthday card; or buying an elaborate stable door long after the horse has bolted.

These ceremonies often are in churches visited only a handful of times in our lifetimes. There, a poem someone once cried over when John Hannah spoke in Four Weddings and a Funeral will be read or a hymn they've never sung but might know as the 'FA Cup song' is mimed to.

Do we ever ask:

Did your Grandad really like poetry?

Did he want a church funeral?

Was he bothered if the coffin that would be burnt anyway was made of mahogany or chipboard?

One undertaker asked, "What sort of coffin would your father have liked?"

"He was in the Navy for years... do you have one with portholes?"

Humour can be found in the darkest of places...

Who are we doing this for? For us? For the deceased? Or is it just the way it's always been? We've seen this at funerals before, so it must be right...

If we applied "It's how we've always done it" to everything, nothing would ever change or improve... we'd still be applying leeches and riding horses.

Funerals are rarely honest...

Little has changed since Victorian times. In many ways, it is as if the world stopped spinning. People sit on uncomfortable pews as a locum member of the clergy reads out rose-tinted stories about a person they never met. It's how we've always done it so why change, as another dirge of organ music is played out of time by someone who sounds as if they don't want to be there?

All too often, services seem distanced... lacking detail or connection. Some appear to be generic exercises - "add name of the deceased here". Crematorium services consist of entering one door to exit another like a conveyor belt of grief without a cuddly toy in sight. Then everyone trots off to a nearby pub for curly sandwiches and sausage rolls as people get drunk at the wake. We need to ensure the time in between fits the guest of honour.

One service I attended featured the eulogy, "Vince hated hoovering but liked peanuts. Let us sing hymn 27, The Lord is My Shepherd." Not the most elaborate pen picture I have encountered.

Then again, no vicar ever said, "Dearly beloved, as you all are aware, Alfie was a liar, cheat, womaniser, drunk, wife-beater with 11 kids by 411 unfortunate women! Well, he's off to Hell; good riddance to bad rubbish! Who fancies a beer?"

Instead, many receive magnolia send-offs reading like an unconvincing reference from a boss who was about to sack you before you decided to leave. Perhaps a big seat should be reserved at the back for hypocrisy.

People who have committed suicide are passed off as dying of pneumonia for an otherwise-forbidden Catholic burial. Similarly, eulogies like "Chris was a lifelong friend to Mark. They were as close as brothers" sweep true love under a carpet. All of this is so out of kilter with the times we live in to 'protect' others. Pure hypocrisy. Surely love is love.

Until recently, religion seemed to have a monopoly on death.

"Having our faith meant so much to us for. Our vicar married us, christened our children and came back to the village to do Michael's funeral. It meant so much to us."

Thankfully, more people are making the ceremony fit the person and their wishes these days.

Andy Hamilton in his film "What We Did On Our Holiday" highlighted the importance of respecting wishes and the value of the relationships between children and grandparents, as the so-called decision-maker generation in between often get everything wrong while trying to do the right thing to appease onlookers. The burning Viking boat funeral would never have entered the thoughts of the 'grown-ups'.

In this research, I have encountered people with learning disabilities excluded from being present at their mother's funeral because 'it might upset her'. Is this the real reason?

People love to say what is in a person's best interest without ever asking or having asked. We need to ensure our wishes are known and carried out. That is respect, dignity and care.

Children often aren't given the opportunity to attend funerals… why? If not included, are they excluded? How can we include them to help them grieve, too?

I have a memory for detail yet cannot remember much from funerals of those of whom I truly love, only that they weren't as bad as I'd expected. I wasn't really there. I sent my body to fill a suit.

No matter how many funerals I attend, it doesn't seem to get any better.

One interviewee, after a life of mix and match religion -

"A bit Muslim, Christmas is fun, Ramadan keeps my weight down, etc." He found himself at a crash course in preparing a father's body on his hardest day - his own father's funeral. He had no clue that this was what happened at a Muslim funeral. He had never been to one before.

He wasn't at his most receptive. He wasn't prepared. A little boy in a man's body. Rehearsing with a full theatre.

Elsewhere, someone deemed it appropriate to have young Princes William and Harry walk down the streets of London following their mother's coffin. "Put them in a car!" I shouted at the television in an empty room. "Why do they have to walk with the weight of the world's eyes on them?"

Funerals are also the worst place to want to laugh… all it takes is one memory to make you lose control. Shockingly, the most undignified thing I have seen at a funeral was by elected dignitaries, who should be a point of reference in etiquette and protocol sat together taking selfies at a state funeral. Presidents and prime ministers playing with mobile phones when we ask children to check them in at the school reception: unbelievable!

What if an ex dies? This is a difficult one…

The hatchet has often been buried and forgotten. Once you loved them and you may be upset. But should you go? Is that disloyal? What is the right thing to do?

If they are not "immediate close family" then employers might not allow you to attend. Friends aren't "really close family". Many are closer.

This situation once led to a deputy head teacher saying, after 38 years' loyal and blemish-free service, that they could "shove their job" after he was refused permission to attend a life long friend's funeral.Funnily enough, after a short reflection, the new-in-post headteacher let him attend.

Nobody wants to see their Dad cry; their hero; their point of reference; the man who grabbed you from over-ambitious trees; the man with all the answers clutching only questions in his hand.

Funerals are tough. Weddings see guests spending weeks choosing just one hat. Sadly, some guests at funerals are forced to wear two - playing both father and son or mother and daughter. It is hard to grieve while consoling someone else.

During flight safety demos on planes, the voice says: "Put on your own oxygen mask before putting your children's on." This is often greeted by an aggressive, disdainful display of meerkat-style necks rising between the headrests as mothers wonder if the cabin crew has made a mistake.

Perhaps that is why many people elect not to take children to funerals. Not for the good of the children, but for the good of the adults. This then sends an odd message to the children. How are they meant to get their heads around grief if the adults they turn to for guidance cannot do so themselves? We need to start this conversation.

Are funerals an 18, 15, 12, PG or a U certificate? At that point, the parents aren't usually in a best place to offer guidance.

My mother-in-law lives with dementia and every time a favourite song comes on the radio, she says: "What's this one again? I'd like this played at my funeral."

"Liz, your playlist is so big, your funeral will be like Live Aid with a box!"

One woman who had never left the street where she lived for 40 years because of agoraphobia, planned and timed her husband's funeral to the minute with meticulous care. She had a neighbour read the lesson and eulogies, then they stood and sang the hymns at the same time, with her playing the out-of-tune piano. This mattered so much to her. She loved him so much. She said goodbye in her way in private.

Albert was 103 when his young wife Betty, 98, died. A fantastic, bright man, virtually blind and with only one ear barely functioning. He was unable to write a eulogy for the vicar, who did not know his Betty, so I offered to help him write one with his niece. We enjoyed a cup of tea together talking about his wife and his fond memories of them eloping in their forties. We laughed as I took rough notes. I went away and typed them up and read it back to him.

"That's champion, lad. Perfect."

My heart was full as he shook my hand with a century of life still pulsing through him. Our words were read at the intimate funeral held at a table in a church. The vicar sat next to Albert's good ear as the three other invited members of the congregation eavesdropped.

"She was too beautiful for me, lad!"

"I think she did pretty well, too."

At some stage a bit of dust may have got in my eye…

We wouldn't wear shoes that don't fit us so why do it with a funeral? The only way to ensure all wishes are respected is to ask long before instead of rolling a dice after they have gone.

Respect

"Spike isn't moving Dad. He's spread out like a starfish with his eyes open but he hasn't blinked once. Can you come and check."

The joys of fatherhood… Today as well as taxi driver and homework checker I was about to debut as a coroner.

Annie would have moved him as she was scared of nothing but wanted me to do it.

Spike was rock solid and fat as a pampered Pekinese despite only ever living on salad!

I noted the time of death but realised it must have happened much earlier in the day.

She desperately needed to know he was definitely dead. We had to be certain and that he wasn't going to wake up in a box tapping on the underside of the lid. She had heard horror stories of tortoises waking up from hibernation buried alive in shoeboxes.

Annie was bereft despite never ever offering to clean out his plastic home or change his sawdust.

She couldn't stop crying. I thought let's get her off to sleep then we'll dispose of the body under the cloak of darkness.

This organic fly-tipping was not an option. I was about to learn about respect and dignity from my 10 year old.

At a scene of a crime they put casualties in plastic bags - this wasn't good enough for our guinea pig.

"I can't imagine him in a bin like another piece of rubbish." Annie said.

Her head wasn't going to hit a pillow without us doing what was right for our little furry friend who spent many a night snuggled in a towel on her lap watching mind-numbing reality TV.

She couldn't let him stay in the summer house overnight.

us as a going away present to help him on his way. I was then given strict instructions to place him gently , the right way up and to wrap him in one of our best clean fluffy towels-Mum would have normally reacted unfavourably to this choice of linen but turned a blind eye out of respect.

We moved his little brother inside and cuddled him enveloping him in attention to hopefully distract from his loss-if only temporarily. We contacted our friend who had a smallholding and set off with the coffin in the back of our black Volvo 4x4. I even drove carefully as if driving a hearse.

Annie insisted this had to be done immediately-more urgent than a Jewish funeral!

We discussed the difficult choice between cremation or burial en route?

"Grown ups use the word CREMATION but it's still just burning isn't it? Just putting them on a fire.

I think it's better for them - they go up and aren't trapped in a box - that's horrible - both are awful but one gives off light and warmth - the other is cold and dark and lonely.

Then he'll go up for a party up in heaven - he'll be alright.

She wouldn't allow him to stay in the car overnight in case I went to work the next day and forgot about my silent passenger.

She ensured that his little brother Captain Rex was protected from the situation and was cuddled and comforted. He must have been laid next to his motionless brother for most of the day. Who knows what he was thinking...

She cleaned out his cage in case of germs.

Then she set about creating a coffin worthy of him. An empty UGGS box for a pair of overpriced sheepskin boots fitted the bill perfectly.

Annie drew pictures on the outside and wrote a beautiful message from

I'm sad for his brother.

I'm sorry he can't speak to us. He can't tell us how he feels. How upsetting must that be. We'll have to give an extra special eye to him to see if he needs us.

All he can do is eat more parsley or move about quicker.

All we can do is talk to him nicely, be there for him and give him cuddles to let him know we're there for him."

We left him with our friend who can talk to the animals better than Doolittle or Tarzan who gets on better with animals than people.

She would do the right thing. She had lost so many furry friends over the years. She would show him the respect and dignity he deserved.

"So is it a good idea for children to have pets?"

"It gives us a sense of responsibility like we're someone's parents -it's like having a job but a really nice job. We care for them - make them happy and learn a lot along the way. They're not toys or playthings or a silly little tamagotchi beeping in your pocket.

They are our friends who can't answer back.

But no more pets for me any time soon. Some people want a brand new one straight away.

I need time. This was so much worse than Tom the goldfish. You can't stroke a fish. How do people cope when they lose a cat or a dog?"

"We've done the right thing there tonight."

"Thanks Dad. You don't realise how much you love someone until they're gone."

If this had been left to a "grown-up" how different would this have been?

Why don't we ask children more often?

It Ain't Over 'til It's Over

Imagine being a fly on the wall, able to hear what people really say when you're not in the room. I always question the wisdom of a jealous husband checking his wife's mobile - what are they hoping to find?

"My husband's fantastic! What a lovely man he is! I'm truly blessed, to share my life with such a trusting soul."

There's a greater chance of it being terrible and blowing up in their face, but imagine turning up to your own funeral...

Sooty had been diagnosed with stage four bowel cancer five years ago. His attitude and approach to this was unmistakably him. He would use all the drive, energy, enthusiasm and optimism, which he was known for, to face it FULL ON and FIGHT IT.

He almost won.

Four years into his treatment he was due a visit to his consultant and was hoping for his third all clear in a row. This appointment came just three days after completing a 100km charity bike ride with his eldest son.

He had taken the chemo and experienced some serious pain, both mentally and physically. He had invaluable support from his partner Natalie, children Ella and Jordan and friends. He had gone back to work for a while and we all started to believe that he could beat this cruel disease.

Sadly it wasn't to be as the cancer had returned and spread to his major organs and lymph glands around his body. It wasn't looking good for Sooty so his response was to hold a "Life Party" towards the end of November and continue to fight as he still had HOPE and was lobbying to be included for "Experimental Treatment" for research purposes.

"What the hell is a Life Party?" his friends asked.

He had read about this concept and felt it was perfect for him to bring everyone together from his schooldays through his York Scooter club adventures when he was a young man to present day. By his own admission he was a bit of a lad with a twinkle in his eye and that's why he was so well liked and fun to be with.

Over the years Sooty he had progressed to Senior Management and was very well respected within his company with a loyal circle of friends from all walks of life and of every age such was his personality and charisma.

Once he had explained the concept we "got it" straight away and agreed it was "Pure Sooty".

So one Sunday evening, he took over a city centre pub for the celebration. A memorial with a difference, for one night only. This wasn't Status Quo or Fleetwood Mac, saying it was their last ever tour to peddle tickets... Honestly, this was it!

The pub hid their fire risk assessments in the drawer for the night and arranged to bring in a pa system to reach each floor; no church could have accommodated such numbers without butter and shoehorns. It was standing room only, so tightly packed that some cultures would have demanded people be married soon after!

He got to see his own funeral and be that fly on the wall. Like Randal and Hopkirk (NOT deceased), he was able to enjoy that out-of-body experience and hear what people really thought. Could he be the luckiest man ever, even though he was dying? He'd never felt more alive!

Is this not a better way? If we know someone is dying, why not invite them to the party instead of throwing it without them? It's surely a proper celebratory testimonial if they're there. Love is to be shared whilst we're here, not after we've died. Why aren't more funerals held on an evening? More people could turn up - and it wouldn't cause friction at work.

He got to kiss, cuddle and show his true appreciation to everyone who mattered in his life.

It was more 'This Is Your Life' than 'This Is Your Death'.

Sharing aspects of an American style roast, with wind-ups and funny anecdotes resembling best men's speeches from all of his brothers, from other mothers and his special maids of honour. People said what they truly thought, with not a psalm or hymn number in sight.

He was left in no uncertain terms how loved he was, how much impact he had made, and that he had 'permission' to retire.

The world may be missing a trick here. This was a stunning, bespoke event that fitted him like a Savile Row suit.

Why don't more people throw a leaving party and celebrate a life together?

Why make do with something final when we can have a FINALE?

Relight My Fire

Miss Hobson was married to her job. A once-strict headteacher, she knew she was dying, so decided to put on a special afternoon for "her ladies" who lived in the same care home. I was a regular face as trainer to the care staff, so I was asked if I would accompany them to a function room at a nearby pub for afternoon tea. I felt honoured.

After an exquisite three-tiered array of confectionery that would have met with Mary Berry's approval, in walked three fire-fighters, without knocking. Strangely, no fire alarms had been sounded. Perhaps they were there for an inspection - but it was odd for them to be in full fire-retardant attire and helmets...

and why did it need three of them to inspect such a small village pub? This seemed like cracking a nut with a sledgehammer.

Then, suddenly, I realised I may have been the most qualified firefighter in the room as Tom Jones' "You Can Leave Your Hat On" blasted through the speakers, interrupting this twee and tweedy Headmistress spinster's soiree with her 90-year old friends.

Conversation about how lovely the scones were stopped as their attention was stolen by our gate-crashers. Their hoses exposed...

This was a straight-laced lady's last taste of outrageousness! I didn't know where to look! They did! Who'd have thought it of Miss Hobson?

Bucket list ticked! Glasses raised. All fires still ablaze! Not extinguished just yet...

We Are Family

Janine knew she was dying, as did everyone else. She wanted to celebrate her life, so a band of musicians were assembled, especially to play her favourite songs. Everyone there knew their reason for attending, so nobody needed to mention it. Nobody was staring down morosely at their shoes - they were too busy dancing! Good company, good eating, singing together... An imminent "Last orders!" and "Time, gentlemen, please!" was coming, but there were glasses to be raised before then.

Janine wanted a party on borrowed time. She witnessed her daughter get up with the band and play Imagine on the piano; she was so proud, holding her daughter so closely, the whole family together. Once again, some dust may have got in our eyes...

Sometimes adversity can create a watertight siege mentality - a hand grenade couldn't separate them.

Just 24 hours after Janine's funeral, her family walked bravely and proudly onto York Barbican stage and explained what St. Leonard's Hospice meant to them.

They all held hands - united - when one struggled to get their words out another stepped in and took the microphone. They stood as one - all hurting - all together - but definite they were going to get each other through it. A beautiful, powerful, moving display of what family means.

I wonder if they even noticed the 1500 people in front of them. As part of "A Night to Remember", they helped raise £37,000 in one night. A stunning send off, to show the power of family, the power of togetherness and the love for a wife, sister and mother of whom they were so very very proud.

The Leader Of The Pack

"Hello, Ian. It's Eleanor," said the unfamiliar voice on the phone.

I needed nothing else; I predicted the rest. Why was she calling? If Steve and her had split up, he'd be calling.

Like a death knell sounding, this was not good news. The emotion hit me before she finished. Pricey's heart had run out of beats. He died instantly. Unpredictable to the last.

Steve lived fast... volume turned up to distortion. The only thing he did in moderation was moderation! Never went steady - his Scalextric trigger finger on full for every corner.

Despite rarely seeing each other, we both knew we were always there to put the world right. A special man. My big regret was that, for the previous six months, we had kept trying to get together - but didn't. People less important prevented that from happening - a lesson learnt too late.

"Steve thought a lot of you. Will you speak at his funeral?"

"Definitely!"

"And will you do something else?"

I thought she was going to ask me to carry him with his friends and brothers. Heavy lifting wasn't a problem...

"Will you sing his favourite song: 'Fields of Gold'?"

This was heavier lifting than I was expecting! I paused, took a couple of long breaths, then said "Of course. It'll be an honour."

I have always said that singing isn't hard, but in this case I could not have been more wrong.

I put the phone back in my pocket and felt a strange, warm energy hit me, giving me an odd boost. As if Pricey had sent it for me as a parting gift as it was of no use to him anymore. This made such an impression on me, I picked up this book again and continued writing.

I felt full. Could it be magic? It felt real to me.

I had sung to full auditoriums before. Surely I'd be fine...? But there was no Take 2. All I could think of was seeing Elton John sweat, singing his revamped "Candle in the Wind". I played the song on guitar at home then opted for a backing track to reduce the variables to go wrong. I took two days off work, unpaid, to rehearse four minutes that needed to be right. Good enough wasn't good enough for my mate. Not once did I reach the end in one piece.

I was driving myself sixty miles across the Pennines to the funeral so didn't have the luxury of Dutch courage. I remembered the words of a colleague: "I only go to funerals of people I don't really care about. Otherwise it's too hard." I thought the world of Pricey. He was a one-off - hilarious and unpredictable.

Sat in my car to avoid the rain I arrived nearly two hours early.

"If I arrive late I waste your time; if I arrive early I waste mine."

It was better for me to be there in plenty of time. The men at the crematorium saw I was at a loose end and invited me 'backstage'.

"So what's the difference between burning and cremation?"

"You can survive a burn - you don't survive cremation!"

Old hips don't burn, mobile phones go in, jewellery, watches... Egyptian Mummies went in with fewer extras.

The men who worked there had dignity and respect at the centre of everything they did, ensuring they got everything right with the care of a midwife.

I saw four funerals come and go where exquisite floral tributes went in the front door then were thrown out into the green bins to be mulched within half an hour. They could have made someone else happy, but the box had been ticked and they had outlived their purpose.

Terraces of gravestones stood like the rooftops of a Lowry painting. This was the toughest gig of my life. All nails bitten. All the surrounding skin chewed so my hands were throbbing with a pulse of their own. Talking to myself more than Norman Bates on a stormy night.

I looked on anxiously as dozens of cars arrived, the mourners wearing pale blue and white scarves. I stood alone, detached from the crowd, like an unknown illegitimate son from a dalliance decades ago, skulking at the back trying not to be seen. I had no-one to talk to. I had no idea how many were coming. Then three hundred descended. They were about to fit a quart into a pint pot. All the aisles and perimeters were filled.

"This is the biggest turn out since they cremated Bernard Manning!" remarked one mourner, taking the last drag off his cigarette.

It resembled a funeral for a loveable rogue or a Gypsy King. Many a dubious sick-note had been thrown in for this sell-out matinee. All were here out of love, not duty.

It was a humanist ceremony. The Lord wasn't Pricey's shepherd - nobody was - he was a charming black sheep, whose life's work was to avoid following the flock! The hymn numbers still on the board from the previous service wouldn't refer to Led Zeppelin or Bowie favourites.

Nothing was generic. People 'unaccustomed to public speaking' exceeded all expectations as their hearts overrode their heads, as they waxed lyrical with spellbinding words worthy of any hero. A moving kiss on the coffin or some other acknowledgement turned the congregation into a roomful of people determined not to make eye contact with anyone else for fear of dissolving… We all dissolved!

I focused on the ceiling, the floor, played Countdown with the hymn numbers, played with my beard, rocked from left to right like a

Newton's Cradle trapped in an ill-fitting suit.

I had never been to a funeral like it. This was a true tribute from people who really mattered. I was proud and honoured to stand up in front of two hundred and ninety eight strangers - and Eleanor.

My remit was simple. "Do what Steve would enjoy… You're leaning on an open door, Ian. You'll be fine."

We were allowed to speak in the tongue of our absent friend - we could even go post-watershed with our language!

So I did… and here's my eulogy to Pricey:

In 1992, I started Leeds Met. If he told you he went to Uni, he lied. It was a Poly at best! I walked into a room of not the most interesting people in the world, all wanting to be school teachers… then in walked someone else... in shorts... with long, spindly, flamingo legs, a Colombian drug dealer moustache and a Mancunian swagger... Steve Price.

"Just call me Pricey!"

Instantly we clicked. He was outrageous. He said he was a mature student. He was an IMMATURE student - he was just old!

We were two naughty lads at the back of the class, but he wasn't the class clown. Despite his carefree exterior, he cared. He was clever, conscientious and a phenomenal teacher. He understood kids because in many ways he was one of them, with a different date of birth.

I remember when he finally got with Eleanor he was unbearable, like the cat who got the cream, living every day like it was his last. His amp was always turned up to 11. He danced like no-one was watching.

Pricey doesn't suit being dead. Dead doesn't fit him. We're all expecting him to run in at the back and be the life and soul of the party. The man who only went running so he could drink more beer and eat bigger curries. The man who once showed off "Wild Wood" guitar licks to a guest at a wedding, only to find out the bloke in front of him was Paul Weller's guitarist, Steve Craddock!!! Hilarious!

Pricey had heard of tact but decided against it, often preferring to say out loud what others were thinking, without a filter. Everyone was entitled to Pricey's opinion.

If Pricey was your mate, feel honoured because you have passed the most stringent of "ARSEHOLE" tests known to man.

I remember at my 40th birthday in York, the theme was an '80's school disco with school uniform - the lot!

"Ian, who the hell is that coming in?"

It was Pricey, dressed as a blonde schoolgirl!

My favourite memory is when we once had to hand in a massive assignment one Monday at Uni.

"Steve, where's yours?"

"Sorry, Norah, it was the Beer Walk at the weekend... I was leathered... proper lashed... You'll not be marking all of them today... or tomorrow. I tell you what, you crack on marking them and by Friday, you'll have got through most of them... then I'll stick mine on the top, still warm, ready to go."

"But, Steve…"

"Norah… DIMDIF."

"DIMDIF? Stephen, what's that?"

"DOES IT MATTER? DOES IT F##K…"

Pricey knew what DIDN'T matter.

Pricey knew who DIDN'T matter.

But Pricey showed us that WE mattered.

That is why there is only one word for how we feel today…

PRICELESS!

The room laughed and cried as one. In five minutes, I had become their friend. I told them I had been asked to do something else, but admitted I had a 0% success record so far, so I asked them all to close their eyes and think of the things they loved most about our absent friend.

I had never felt expectation like this before.

I was about to encounter Emotional Binary - either I could do this or I couldn't - nothing in-between. No rehearsal had helped even though I had taken 48 hours to rehearse 224 words! It was like walking out at Wembley to hear "Abide with me", unsure if I could kick the ball or if I would freeze.

I sang "Fields of Gold" for my friend with my voice cracking only once. I think he would let me off. I have never felt happier getting to the end of a song.

The congregation applauded as I nodded in respect and made my way to the back of the crematorium. As everybody left, strangers shook my hand and hugged me, all in City scarves despite many of them being ardent United fans.

The congregation left to "Stairway to Heaven". I couldn't help but smile, thinking of some of our nights out when "Highway to Hell" may have been more appropriate!

"Please will you join us for a few beers back at the pub?" asked Eleanor.

"I've got to drive home. Bless ya."

"Well, have a sit down and a think for five minutes before you set off."

I walked back to my car with all the baggage I'd arrived with checked in. I felt a huge relief. Opening the car door, I sat down and cried and cried with the release of pressure. Mission accomplished, and I'm still standing.

I still felt honoured during the journey back over the M62 as I reflected on the day. It will be a very long time before I can even begin to think of my mate as no longer being at the end of the phone. His mobile number still sits within my contacts.

Occasionally, we meet people who make it worth pushing yourself to possible failure. Even if I'd had messed up, Pricey would have just said "DIMDIF!" and thanked me for trying.

There Is A Light That Never Goes Out

Love is a selfish emotion. We are with people because of how they make us feel. When we lose them, who do we really cry for?

We cry for us. We cry for all we have lost. We cry for the perfect life we never really appreciated. Every day we spend with somebody is another day we are ill prepared to not have them. We love people to death... and often beyond.

"In sickness and in health, 'til death us do part..." - maybe longer.

Dame S. Saunders said: "You matter 'til the day you die... many matter afterwards."

Meet the love of your life... She's beautiful, funny, happy and a joy to be around. She makes your heart beat faster than you could imagine and your smile so broad your face can barely accommodate it. After meeting her, you won't want to spend another day apart.

Then something changes...

At some stage, you'll become her domestic nemesis; she'll spend her life complaining about insignificant stuff (in your eyes), such as socks missing in the wash-basket, toast crumbs left on the work surface, chomping while eating and watching Newcastle United play yet again, even though "you watched them just last week".

Every couple you see arguing in a supermarket, or niggling over nothing, at some point worshipped each other, would once sneak out of the back door early for a date and come back late to meet the wrath of their parents.

Yet at some point, over time, their focus goes from everything they adored about their partner to the things that infuriate, turning from Romeo and Juliet to Sherlock Holmes and Moriarty.

'Perfect' Mills and Boon relationships have arguments, squabbles, warring words splattered on a canvas of love. Sometimes people miss the stuff that pushed their buttons. I was told by one interviewee that: "Arguing shows you're bothered."

We are creatures of habit. As physios talk about 'muscle memory', we are reminded that the heart is a muscle too.

"Hi Honey, I'm home." He walks through the door the same as he always does, except his wife is no longer alive to answer. As the words leave his lips, he is heartbroken all over again.

If you asked many couples "What winds you up? What tugs at your coat?" they often focus on the person they have chosen to live every remaining day of their life with as a source of their irritation - for better for worse, in sickness and in health, 'til death us do part.

All of the things that wind you up, you may miss if they were stolen from you.

Many carry on doing the same things. Some still make two cups of tea and say "Sorry, dear" as they break wind on the settee. Some buy dog food long after the pet has died, and end up donating it to the RSPCA, just to feel as if nothing has changed.

"I still put on Match of the Day, even though I hate it!"

"I never thought I would miss his snoring in his armchair. We tried everything. We even did separate bedrooms! Now it's gone, I'd kill to be woken up by it tonight. I now sit in that armchair now deafened by the quiet."

"Driving is tediously calm without his hapless manoeuvres and shocking parking."

"Being able to finish off my own sentences isn't as satisfying as I remember."

142

"I never thought I'd miss her getting her words wrong - state of the ark, black forest grotto, not of the same elk... I even miss her being pacific!"

"I hate having a spotless house - no socks or wet towels lying around. I didn't want no mess, I just wanted less mess. Nobody leaves mugs on the bedside table or puts the butter knife in the jam, nobody puts back bottles of milk with only a drop in the bottom, wees on the seat, or leaves the toilet looking like Hockenheim..."

One interviewee says "Goodnight" to a photo of his wife at the bottom of the stairs; the picture frame wears her necklace with her name on it. How many people continue the conversation in an empty house, playing both roles? Many think it's just them; I'm sure it's not.

We're not talking to imaginary friends - these are real.

One care worker commented about a man she cared for: "Frank calls out in the night for no reason." No! He calls out for a reason.

One woman always says in B&Bs: "I hope you have plenty of pillows." Unknown to the proprietor, she has slept for past 19 years with three pillows plumped up by her side, to fill the void her husband left. Imagine if the last thing you said to the love of your life was about socks missing the wash basket and not "I love you."

When someone dies, you lose cuddles, going out together, mutual friends (who, you may realise, were more your wife's friends than yours), conversation and possibly the reason you get out of bed every morning.

One of my friends - a brilliant teacher and a practical man who adored his wife - was unable to speak in his last days so he wrote down what really mattered on a piece of paper just before he died:

"MOT July 7th

Love you xxx"

It summed him up. He knew his wife would never remember important stuff like the MOT and the thought of her driving around uninsured was destroying him. He left her in no doubt about what mattered - and how much he truly thought of her.

"I'd give anything for another argument with you!"

We love a nemesis. I'm sure George loved Mildred, despite everything he said.

Sometimes, we only fully appreciate someone after they have gone. Think how many 'Oscars' and Lifetime Achievement Awards are given to performers long after they have taken their final bows.

We don't miss them on bad days, because we wouldn't want to trouble or burden them; it's on the days when you desperately want to call them to share some fantastic news, or to tell them the joke that has reduced you to tears.

Throughout life, we replace things. Our favourite shoes soon go from Cinderella to 'binderella' once they've outlived their comfort. Workmates come and go, boyfriends are upgraded to better looking, funnier, sportier versions. But we rarely replace those we have loved.

Even when new relationships begin, the new partner is not a substitute. Rarely do people replace like with like, a human new-for-old insurance policy. We don't use the old love and split it in two. It's like when you have another child; their inheritance may have just halved, but you suddenly generate twice as much love to go around.

Yvonne Richmond-Tunnock's husband died, but she kept his surname when she married again, so as not to have 'divorced' him. People die, but the relationship lives on.

One interviewee told me: "I'm still married, but my husband passed away in 1979." So poignant, yet true. She is 96, but never wanted anyone else. She had found 'the one'. He died; the love did not. His life is like a maypole that she dances around with every sentence. What he did, what he said, what he thought is quoted in her every conversation. What he'd think of something happening today. It's as if he never left. Such an unconditional love, he didn't even need to be alive. Perhaps that's why she's still married.

"It's hard to write new chapters if you're busy re-reading the old ones." (Dear Dementia by ID) but if they're the stories you love, they can be re-read and quoted from many times.

Bob Monkhouse once said: "No happy marriage can end well." The sentiment was reinforced by songwriter Dan Webster: "Time will break one of our hearts."

One widow, Val, forgets about the rules of English language. She starts most sentences with "Ken…" and ends them with a smile. Each reference keeps him close. She looks at everything as if his eyes can still see too, and listens as if he can still hear. A life-long love affair that has long outlived him. He is still with her everywhere and every day, though his body is somewhere else. He hasn't really left her. Val believes that, as do I. Anecdotes and answering questions - She carries on playing both parts. It helps.

"Don't make me close one more door, I don't wanna hurt anymore… Stay in my arms if you dare.

Personal announcements
to place an announcement please 01904 676767

Rest In Peace

Must I imagine you there?

Don't walk away from me!

I have nothing, nothing, nothing, if I don't have you."

(I Have Nothing by Linda Thompson)

Sinatra sang: "Saturday night is the loneliest night of the week" but, based on our interviewees, Sunday nights pip it to the post. Esther Rantzen said: "It is easy to find people to do things with, but it is difficult to find someone to do nothing with." Sometimes people feel most alone in company as if they have nothing in common any more. The plus one, the odd sock, the also ran...

The barbecue rusts in the garden, the caravan is a shrine to holidays past, gathering moss on the drive. You can go out whenever you want but who would you go with? The sad truth is that even on a perfect day, you only have half of what you had.

Life would be so much easier if Barry Manilow had recorded "I CAN smile without you" and Bill Withers had had a hit with "There'll be sunshine when she's gone..."

Any couple would ideally want to die at the same time. I've often wondered whether men marry younger women not just to pick from the tree rather than the barrel, but also knowing that they won't be left alone, not wanting to be the single playing card trying to stand up unsupported.

Here's a question... What if we added another wedding vow? "To have and to hold, for richer, for poorer, in sickness and in health... and if one dies, you have the option to both go together."

Imagine the impact on society - for better or worse?

Researching this book, I spend three days on my own, wife and kids away, no phone. Loneliness soon gets its claws into me. Time is soon killed, with nothing much to show. Silence isn't the golden commodity you thought it was. Going to sleep in an empty house is not easy.

No "have you brushed your teeth?" on a morning or at night.

No "have you done your homework?"

Throughout life, we wish we didn't have to compromise, that endless give and take. Then, when you can do what you like, you realise it really was always better to give than to receive.

So, next time the conversation goes "Why haven't you cleaned the pan?" followed by "I've put it in the sink to soak...", imagine if they were your last words.

Be careful what you wish for.

Be careful what you whinge for.

That's What Friends Are For

His feet sat up on his comfier version of a dentist's chair - remote control ever-present on the arm, phone in his shirt top pocket as he can no longer rush to answer it in time.

His door is always open as it always was. Just sat there waiting for company to visit his island. Where once he drove everywhere, his car is now somebody's first pride and joy. Where once he could walk for miles, his steps are now limited - his pedometer rarely hits three digits as familiar faces have disappeared.

A memory not as good as it was - making mistakes he'd never make - after a stroke he never noticed he'd had.

Not really sure how good he is these days.

He is the elder of the tribe - the chief - the wisest cleverest man with the most feathers. He has smoked more pipe than anyone else to keep the peace in this village.

"Please can you speak at the funeral?"

A simple throwaway question. He was a gifted speaker. On another day this wouldn't have been an issue but the game has changed. The man they knew isn't the man they see today yet they, somehow, expect the same outcome.

The go to - for help - to do
things they can't handle
and rather than say "I
don't know if I can" he just
says "Yes no problem. Just
tell me the date and time".
Like he always had.

We were terrified. Was
this the point where the
feathers moulted from his
head-dress?

We offered to write it
with him. He ignored any
advice. He knew better.
That's why people asked
him. He always knew
better.

The church was full. The details
were wrong in the order of service.
It came to the time where the
spotlight fell on him - the pulpit
unused as he couldn't scale those
heights as he once did. Just an old
man with a stick - his daughter
playing wicketkeeper hoping her
services wouldn't be needed.

Would he sink or swim? There was
only one way to find out. There was
no dress rehearsal for this. The ad
hoc wooden lectern stood redundant
by his side like an occasional table
because all of his crib sheets were
left covered in toast crumbs by his
breakfast pots. The time arrived
for him to go live on-air without
autocue or safety net not even
the postcards to sweat over like a
terrified best man at a wedding.

They can see he is older. They can
see he is not the man who they have
grown up with.

Silence fell on the congregation.
An uncomfortable pause lasted just
too long then the words came from
somewhere. The delivery came from
somewhere. He made people laugh and
cry as he slowly walked up and down
the aisle stick in hand. Where did
this clarity and flow come from?

He can't remember his tablets any
more or the items on a shopping list
but somehow for one his friends he
remembered what really mattered
when it really mattered.

"I'm ok in the past. It's the present I
struggle with."

Carry On Regardless

We can't choose our parents. As scientists strive ever closer to genetically modify designer babies we have no say in our parents - their ailments, their characteristics or their dates of birth.

He was an afterthought - a surprise - A bonus. A last hussar! The final kick of a dying horse. His parents - more Abraham and Sarah than Mary and Joseph. He had a very different upbringing to his brothers and sisters as they had flown the nest a generation ago.

At Parents Evening people looked on assuming he'd brought Grandma and Granddad.

He lost both of them just months apart. As the second died the shock of the first found him numb. It was like he'd broken both arms, worn a

pot for a day, got it signed by some friends then discharged himself from hospital after ticking the "mended" box.

He was now an 'orphan' - Oliver Twist with the cord finally cut forever. It dawned on him he was nobody's 'little soldier' or No.1 anymore. All branches above him in his family tree had been felled. He had to face the world alone. So he carried on regardless. As you were.

The ashes live in the front room under a table - no clever sculpture, no headstones just constant companions but he rarely sees them as he is always out.

Life became an endless loop of work, pub, bed. Money wasn't a worry but it wasn't a pleasure either. Work wasn't there to pay for life but to fill another day with distraction. His inheritance merely digits on a statement; untouched knowing that as soon as a penny was spent the reality may kick in. His groundhog day existence preventing him from ever acknowledging his losses and start dealing with them.

'Experts' say how you must face your demons head on but he expends all of his energy swerving them. He has decided to turn the other cheek and walk away. A life in denial. Has he got it wrong?

His hop-based regime creates a race to see if head, heart or liver will survive longest. Gallstones make irritating bedfellows.

Every sentence punctuated with three nervous laughs - a coping strategy, yet another distraction.

After two life changing events one would expect to find injuries, exit wounds but it is as if nothing happened - not a scar in sight.

Five years down the line there is "Nothing to see here. Move along."

Smalltalk elastoplasts cover far deeper wounds always swimming down the shallow end for fear of drowning in anything of any depth.

Surrounding himself with people who need him more than he needs them. All previous loves where he adored them; long gone. That will never happen again. He removed that risk - turning a life into a safer existence but all on his terms avoiding all of the world's lows but also missing some of the highs.

Nothing too deep - Spurs, pub quizzes and occasional drunken karaoke but closed heart for fear of breaking. Drunk or sober he never drops his drawbridge. He spends more time berating Sol Campbell than celebrating his parents. Will the reality ever kick in? Is he the first person immune?

He spends so much time icing that he doesn't notice that the cake has gone.

Surrounding himself with upbeat songs in major keys life looks carefree and teflon coated to avoid responsibility.

But we only see him when he's putting another £1 coin on the pool table; the winner who stays on despite losing his two biggest games. The world tells him he should deal with this.

Just because he's in the minority does not necessarily mean he is wrong.

Is he a pressure cooker ? Is he a time bomb? Or has he found his grail for survival? WE do what WE need to do at that time.

Only one person truly knows. We should just be the friend HE wants us to be.

Will we ever scratch the surface? Will he?

The hangover never kicks in if you stay drunk.

149

More Than A Woman

It's strange, but apparently I'm different. I didn't have a big man to teach me how to bowl, or to rescue me from over-ambitious tree climbing. I didn't know I was different, because I didn't know any different. I only ever knew it was just Mum and me.

Everyone else had Dads who turned up at football and Parents' Evenings; I simply thought "We have a cat and they don't." Mum was everything and everyone I needed. Always there first thing in the morning and last thing at night and, strangely, never ill. I assume she slept, but she was always there when my eyes opened.

We did meet but only for twenty three days. I can't imagine seeing my new-born and knowing I will never see them grow up. I have no memory and, perhaps strangely, I've never really asked much about him. This shocks a lot of people. Apparently, I should be more inquisitive. Other people seem to know so much more about how I should be feeling than I actually do myself!

School desperately wanted to "fix" me with counsellors, but I hadn't realised I was broken. Apparently, I should have been fascinated by my ancestry but I didn't want to upset Mum and thought "What good would it do anyway? It won't bring him back!"

We just kept busy; two of us, against the world. Fifty years later I have looked at a few photos and I'm shocked by how much I look like

Dad. I've never grieved, because I never felt I lost anyone. You can only lose something you once had; I only ever gained. Mum faced a situation as horrific as any young mother could imagine and, somehow, created a wonderful life for me - with heart-breaking ingredients.

I'm sure there will have been nights when I lay upstairs, happily dreaming, while she sobbed downstairs, with nobody to comfort her. She always sheltered me from that. Mum put her life on hold; she never bothered with relationships or remarrying - and it was all for me. It was as if she had put a "No Vacancies" sign in the window; there was no room at our inn. She was a one-man woman and I was the one man.

Has not having a Dad affected me? Am I different? Perhaps. I know I sometimes keep a bit of me back, be an island and try not to be too dependent on anyone...

Overall, losing Dad taught me one thing: He chose an amazing woman. My Mum.

Dad would be proud of her.

I am.

You've Got To Hide Your Love Away

Stood at the back ashamed,
hoping nobody notices me but,
secretly, wanting to be noticed.
I'm not mentioned in the order
of service, I'm not family, I'm not
friends. I'm nobody. My Nana would
have called me a scarlet woman. I am
the other woman. The one he came to
to escape his life of mediocrity.

I can't go back to the hotel
afterwards to share stories
without unravelling a man's legacy.
I can't meet his daughters and
grandchildren and say how I knew
their Granddad. It was my job to be
invisible, to not exist, to be off
radar. I've never felt so alone.

I crept in late and left whilst all
still had their backs to me. That was
my goodbye. I never had history but
I had his present.

Today I lost my secret love.

Nobody knew about us.

Nobody ever will.

This sadness is mine and mine alone.

Do You Really Want To Hurt Me?

I was the eldest of three and the only girl. According to the saying "A daughter's a daughter for the rest of your life. A son is a son until he takes a wife."

I was close to Dad. I doted on him, but he was a volatile man. He had a terrible temper. He had his moods and we knew words fit for a building site that, as children, many of my friends hadn't heard before.

Dad liked to be boss - to be in control, in charge of his own destiny and everyone else's if he could. The thought of something removing that power unnerved him, making him unbearable.

When Mum was taken ill with a brain tumour, he realised he couldn't solve this with a clever one-liner, a moment of wisdom or by signing a cheque. This was a place where he was powerless, frustrated and bloody angry about it.

I arranged Macmillan sitters every night then, when Mum went into hospice care, I was there seven days a week as he came and went.

He was angry, violent, paranoid - he thought every beeping text message was about him. In the end, he didn't want any family to visit; we were told his wife wasn't a "peepshow" or

something at the end of the pier. But she was our Mum.

When she died, he said "I've made a list of people to tell."

"I've told them, Dad."

"I bet you stood on a chair in the pub and told everyone, did you?"

He was furious. Angrier than I'd seen in years. He shouted at me as if I was his worst enemy. I wasn't good enough for the soles of his shoes.

We barely spoke. If he lost something, I'd find it for him and he'd tell me that I didn't understand.

"You have no idea!" This was in spite of me going through the ordeal of losing my husband a couple of years previously.

He made it clear, using three F's at the front and end of an exclamation, that I wasn't welcome so I left his life, unable to shed a tear for my Mum or grieve, because he had been so horrible to me.

I sent Christmas cards, Father's Day and birthday cards with messages inside, but never crossed his threshold. It hurt but, through the red mist, he had made his feelings clear and I knew exactly what he thought of me.

His cleaner read one of the cards, while dusting, and told him: "She's crying out for you. Get in touch with her."

I had resigned myself for all ties to be cut permanently, then a message appeared on my answer machine.

"Not seen you for a while. Do you fancy bobbing round?" He spoke in an unusually calm and polite voice, as if nothing had happened.

My husband intervened and said that there needed to be some major apologies to me first.

Dad said he couldn't remember. He couldn't remember? How couldn't he remember such heightened emotions? Such a vitriolic attack on someone he supposedly loved? There was so much hatred and fury in his eyes, his expression, his voice and his vile vocabulary.

I gave him the benefit of the doubt. I forgave. He forgot.

He was lost and alone. The head of the family had lost his head. Some say time is the great healer. Since then, Dad and I are closer than ever. He's still got a temper - and a potty mouth on occasion! - but I love him more than I can say.

Sometimes HURT PEOPLE HURT PEOPLE .

No One Is To Blame

Sometimes we are powerless as we try and find a way to vent our frustration. We may kick the cat when we are angry with the dog. Often those closest to us take the brunt.

Some relationships fall victim to events that happened long before they were even thought of. Paul was born after his older brother had died. The impact of that loss made his father question if it was better to have loved and lost than never loved before resulting in him isolating himself and bringing up his son at arm's length, in a guarded more formal manner - more business partners than father and son - to protect himself from lightning potentially striking twice.

No fault of his own.

Both missed out on so much.

No one was to blame.

This is A Man's World... But It Would Be Nothing Without A Woman Or A Girl

Disclaimer: there are sensitive men in the world, men who can share their inner feelings, men who are demonstrative communicators -but more often it goes like this...

"Hi Dad, how are you?"

"Hello love... I'll put your mother on."

Men are, supposedly, if the press articles often written by men, are to be believed-the stronger sex. Stiff upper lips. Strong, silent types - neither of much use when somebody dies. In many cases, this book may have been bought by a woman for a man who doesn't talk - pressure cookers who rarely cook!

Just because we're better at lifting, more adept at retrieving objects from high shelves and experts at loosening tight jar lids... these things don't make the most accurate barometers of true strength.

In the human race, men often come second!

Many men don't talk. They have best mates, but discuss the "big stuff" with themselves. Men love to talk at length about things that don't really matter. Men talk over beer, where they skirt around umpteen topics to avoid what's really yanking their chain. Men rarely pick up an instruction manual or take advice. Some even turn the female voice off on their satnavs!

As flippant and frothy as this sounds, perhaps men should address these traits? Suicide is the biggest killer in men in their 40s - why?

By that time, you know you're not going to captain England, become an astronaut or a Hollywood action hero. Instead, you might be alright, quite good, not a bad bloke at all - just not who you'd dreamt of being. Some mid-life crises become an end of life crisis.

Women meet up. They talk. Some even listen. Often, family care falls to the women. It takes a special man to be Mum and Dad.

"My brothers didn't want mum to get married again, but Geoff is a lovely man who makes her happy and, let's face it, she wasn't crying on their shoulders!"

Around seventy five men under fifty are widowed in the UK every day, yet widowers are still less likely to ask for help or counselling.

At one bereavement group for young children, I noticed that all of the women sat together and sparked up conversations, whereas the dads watched their children playing together as they tapped on their phones.

How many times did you ask your Mum for the answer to important questions? Mums often have the answer.

Perhaps we need to evolve.

Perhaps we need to find strength from the weaker sex.

Perhaps we need to woman up.

The Ascent of Man

man's physical evolution

man's emotional evolution

that was shocking defending!

Food Glorious Food

Think how many of your favourite memories are based around food; Christmases, holidays, birthdays, weddings. So many happy times have us clutching a fork -breaking bread and raising a glass together.

Think about your favourite meals- most will come with the prefix 'Mum's' , 'Nana's' , 'Granddad's'. Recipes handed down from generation to generation - never cited by any will executor but often more important than any other part of an estate.

These aren't dishes that Gregg Wallace would lust over on Masterchef featuring a 'jus' or a 'coulis'. These are meals made without weighing scales and made with the unique ingredient setting these dishes a class apart: Love.

Cooking is personal, creative and a heartfelt gift. It is so much more than adding things to salt and pepper. To even see my son devour a plate of my house speciality beans on toast (with butter expertly spread to the edges like my Dad used to do) makes my heart sing.

Meals for one only exist because cooking for one is no fun!

Why would you bother? One lady interviewed said that when her husband died she "lost the will to cook." She wasn't a big eater - she just loved to make him happy every day-everything homemade-made from scratch. The best way to a man's heart is through his stomach and she loved to see him polish off every last morsel on his plate then finish the other half she couldn't manage before seeing him fall asleep in his armchair snoring through a satisfied smile.

Even if Tesco have dishes with 'Finest' printed on them, he knew they weren't really. He'd choose his wife's cooking over any Michelin-Starred chef.

Having a partner die can have a devastating impact on your wellbeing. Like a fork in the road, you can focus on your nutrition and wellbeing or put yourself last - living on junk convenience food or not even bothering at all. How many times have we heard, "I've forgotten to eat today"? Good nutrition is vital when we lose someone. It helps immune system, brain function and how we sleep. It can influence how we feel about ourselves and the situation we are in.

We would hope that nowadays cooking duties are shared more equally between the sexes. Feminism happened in 1970s but never really reached parts of the north-east. My Dad was looked after-waited on hand and foot: old school. Bras were burnt for no reason in County Durham other than to have to buy another bra!

When Mam died, all of my Dad's favourite meals went with her like a Pharaoh buried with all of their secrets. She was overprotective in how Dad didn't eat anything spicy - in many ways because she didn't know how to cook it.

Some learn to cook because their partners were stunning in the kitchen. Others learn because they were dreadful and could burn water. Dad didn't want to learn to cook. He wanted to learn to cook like Mam- over-boiling vegetables to within an inch of their lives included so he

conscripted his new kitchen hand George... his George Foreman grill. Mam loved to bake but he's never ventured into the murky waters of pastry.

Instead, he can now do gammon, salmon and ham 'n' eggs. Basically, anything that rhymes! A beautiful tribute to a lady who loved to cook to make her husband feel loved.

He is a creature of habit. His fridge always looks the same, as do his cupboards. He knows what he likes and he likes what he knows. Where once there was only top of the range St. Michael products from Marks and Spencer, Dad has copied everything from Mam apart from her budget. Dad is frugal; unafraid of an Aldi or Lidl bargain. Mam would be horrified at his skinflintery but astonished how far he has come. She'd be very proud.

If I Could Turn Back Time

"We tried to make a difference today but WE FAILED..."

A lovely lady, 75, whose husband died had 'written herself off' to merely exist stationary. She lives in a care home that she doesn't need to live in. She has the most beautiful view from her window but her room is a throng of inoffensive magnolia with a single bed and a bedside cabinet. Not a photo in sight. Not a shred of evidence of who she was, is or will be.

She could have just arrived on Earth without a back story.

Her carers desperately wanted to free her of this self-imposed exile but met a dry stone wall. They played the humour card, the chirpy west country charm card, the 'we're both Mums' card, everything to get her out for the first time in a year but to no avail. She was anxious, concerned and afraid. Every day attached to her armchair is broken only to see sunlight through the clouds of smoke from an occasional sneaky cig clinging to the frame of the back door.

She was wearing a beautiful Rolex bought as a gift from her husband stuck at ten to four.

'It's right twice a day" she joked. The battery needed changing but her life was no longer concerned with time.

"It's not a real one - he got it from a 'tat' shop in Benidorm! He haggled them down to a fiver!"

They realised even changing the battery wouldn't make time a great healer today.

Sometimes we need to realise that we can't turn every NO into a YES.

It is a person's right to give up and give in, fitting a low ceiling on their expectations and wallow in what's left.

People can make their own decisions even if others deem them unwise.

They wished they could have picked that lock today, to help a wonderful lady write a new chapter, but sadly they feared that one page will be copied, pasted, read and re-read without future creative input nor illustration.

"Sometimes I wish I had a magic wand or a time machine to make things better. I know more than I did this morning."

PS. The care staff kept offering days out in more and more creative and tempting packaging and eventually they took her out to the coast and had a fantastic time together.

Never write anyone off.

When Love Breaks Down...

Lou was a DIY whizz - creative, methodical and precise.

Visitors marvelled at what they thought was my handywork, giving me all of the credit with their gender stereotypes, but she was both the brains and the brawn. Plumber, sparkie, chippy and decorator, all in one. She could build or mend anything! Whilst others were out partying, enjoying being single and in their early 20s, she registered for every evening class going - and they paid off. She measured three times then cut once. A millimetre out was never good enough.

"If it's not right, it's wrong!"

She planned it, measured it and built it whilst I watched, baked cakes and brought her lots of cups of tea! Whilst my friends had wives who were impossible to buy for, Lou was easy - a 24-volt, industry standard drill, a jig-saw, rawl plug stocking fillers, a toolbelt, anything the Screwfix catalogue had on special offer... She was never one for D&G whilst B&Q was just ten minutes along the ring road.

Her day job couldn't have been further removed from her dirty weekends - she led a team of accountants, crunching numbers, hunting the elusive zero. She thrived on detail and being in control.

We had everything and we shared everything, as equals. We both worked hard and played even harder. Everything money could buy, we bought! Champagne income, but with champagne tastes! Our disposable income was always disposed of! Every weekend or bank holiday could have had a 'before' and 'after' picture. Our home was unrecognisable from the shell we had bought - a total metamorphosis of extensions, conversions, gazebos and sheds.

She was my best friend in the world, who just happened to be gorgeous.

Then from nowhere, without warning, our lives changed forever. Lou's mother died. We adored her and she had loved our bones in return. She'd do anything to see us happy; she was the second best mum in the world!

I can't really remember from school Biology lessons what a pancreas does; all I know is that when they go wrong, they don't hang around.

Lou seemed surprisingly fine about it, very matter of fact and in control as always. She never cried once. I tried to help her cry, but there was nothing! I cried more than she did! No sleepless nights, no breakdowns, no wanting to get drunk and talk rubbish into the early hours - nothing. It was as if it hadn't happened at all. Lou just switched into work mode, where she could be in control.

"I'm too busy to fall to bits. Stuff to do. I'll sort it!"

She quickly made one of her famous lists. (I'd even bought her a hoodie one Christmas with 'I LOVE LISTS' on the back!)

"Newspaper announcement - tick.

Make sure Dad's always got someone with him - tick.

Inform all family - tick.

Sort funeral - tick.

Flowers & caterer - tick.

Solicitors - tick.

Everything that anyone else would overlook -tick."

She was a machine, untouched by emotion. Was her Mum just another one of her projects? I said afterwards that we should take some time off and get away from everything; I was scared she would burn out.

"Got too much on at work. It's everybody's end of year. I need to be there. The boss can't cry off."

Monday arrived. Lippy on, suit on, off she went - as if nothing had happened. But then, gradually, things started eroding... I tried everything I could to help. I cooked her favourite supper, but it was picked at, half-eaten. I offered to give her a magic shoulder rub but, for the first time ever, it was declined. I booked weekends away to the coast, only to have to cancel them at the last minute.

"I don't feel like it."

I sent flowers to her work. Endless offers of "Shall we meet up for lunch?" I soon realised the best I could be was a temporary distraction and at worst, a constant irritant. The girl I had fallen in love with was disappearing fast.

You hear on the news of natural disasters... how many dead and how many casualties. It dawned on me that despite only one fatality, WE were the casualties; innocent victims.

It wasn't my fault.

It wasn't hers.

It wasn't her Mum's.

We had no one to blame. No scapegoat to hate.

"It's not you. It's me."

To the rest of the world we were 'business as usual'.

No arguments.

No fallouts.

Just nothing else.

Nothing.

Conversation soon became stilted. Uncomfortable silences.

"How was work?"

"Fine."

The End.

Not wanting to talk about anything that mattered, we had less and less in common as the clock ticked on. Life was work, then telly, then bed and repeat... When I came in to sit down, she would often get up to make a cup of tea or go and walk the dog without me. If I suggested that we walk him together, she'd make up something she had to do. We went from sharing everything to sharing a laundry basket and a tube of toothpaste. The bed split perfectly in half, as if she'd measured it. My tailor-made cuddles no longer fitted. I was desperate to heal her, to get her back, but my magic powers had disappeared. All affection was rejected, refused...

"This hurts like nothing else. It's MINE! YOU'RE not in it! YOU can't help me! YOU don't understand. YOU don't get it! YOU'VE still got your mother."

I was out in the cold, an outsider in my own home. Within a single second, the person whose every sentence I could finish turned into a total stranger. Her eyes were empty, her heart was cold.

Then she started falling asleep on the sofa, even avoiding venturing upstairs, getting up early and leaving for work with no kiss goodbye.

She lost her mum; I lost my wife. There were no winners, only losers.

Both of us were sitting on a see-saw, neither of us was enjoying the view.

She had run out of lists and had no more projects to create. Just like being at work, she was striving to reach zero.

Where once it had all been about what we had in common, now it was all about our one difference. Once equals, the harsh inequality of life had forced her to leave everything she had created.

Me still having my Mum must have felt as if I was rubbing her nose in it. She couldn't see that we were all in her corner, wanting to mend the cuts, take the blows but in the end she threw in the towel.

Her absence from family get-togethers was noticed, even though I covered for her with an array of excuses and white lies.

"I'll stay in. I've got stuff to do."

She'd never brought work home before.

"I'm off out for a run."

I couldn't remember how she used to be... Lou was becoming a distant memory. Then one day...

"I'm off."

She left.

It was weeks before I told anyone; I was ashamed, afraid, alone. I even kept it from my folks, but they knew. It hit them too, to see everything we had worked so hard for crumble around us. Paddy McAloon said it perfectly:

"When love breaks down,

The things you do, to stop the truth from hurting you.

When love breaks down,

The lies we tell...

They only serve to fool ourselves."

She made the only change she could. She had nobody else; she wanted nobody. Nothing made her happy any more. Sadly, the only person she would have listened to wasn't there. I wish they had phones in heaven.

Sometimes, no matter how much someone loves you, no matter how much they'd like to share your pain, how much they'd love to take your place, you have to DO IT YOURSELF.

165

Lonely This Christmas

"'Tis the season to be jolly", apparently, as the shops fill with mistletoe, matchmakers and Mariah Carey...

...but so many people dread it.

Christmas has the magnifying glass set at its most powerful. If you're happy, you appear happier - but if you have any cracks, Christmas is like frost, getting in there to make it the loneliest day of the year.

One less present to wrap. One less to open. No cards to write. Decorations left in the loft, gathering dust; they were always a two-man operation - and who would you put them up for anyway?

"On Christmas Day, I just want to get up late walk the dog and go to bed early. Santa doesn't visit my house any more. Christmas is past. There's no Christmas present. Bah, humbug."

"Christmas is for kids. Christmas is cancelled. Four walls, heating on full, Iceland meal for one - and yet another repeat of Del Boy and Rodney dressed as Batman and Robin."

We always did Christmas for Mam and Dad at our house so we dreaded the first Christmas without her. We took a long run up from November, like Evel Knievel jumping over the Grand Canyon, secretly knowing we wouldn't make the other side.

We tried to keep busy. The day itself was a feast of food, family and frivolity. The kids enveloped Granddad in love and Lego from breakfast to bedtime. We concentrated so much on not falling to pieces that we got to the end of the day, full and exhausted - then I realised we'd been so busy, and kept Dad so happy, that we hadn't thought of Mam all day! I was angry with myself. How dare I enjoy the day so much without her? Then I took a step back and thought "What Christmas would Mam have wanted us to have today?"

We'd just had that Christmas Day, based on the plans in her handbag. Mam loved Christmas and she'd have loved this one. Mission accomplished.

A year later, I thought we had Christmas sussed, then from nowhere

I fell to pieces before we'd opened a single present! No warning given; it just hit! The ghost of Christmases past, filled with joy, Asti Spumante parading as champagne and Action Men with eagle eyes came to haunt me. Never think you have it sussed.

One Saturday in November, my son Billy got talking to a gentleman at a dementia café, asking what he had planned for Christmas.

"Nothing. It's just me. My wife died and my sons have good jobs and live abroad."

"No-one should have no-one, Peter," said my nine year old, with a considerably older head fitted to his shoulders.

On the journey home, he asked "So, what are we going to do about this then, Dad?"

We got talking in the car and all agreed to try and solve this problem for people living alone in the city. That's when we came up with Xmas Presence - and a monster was created!

It was time to include those people who were outside the loop. No matter how many Facebook groups, websites or Twitter accounts there are, we will not get these... it takes people to say "Hello" and start a conversation.

Word spread like wildfire around the city about Xmas Presence, a project to include those who are alone at Christmas. We now get to spend Christmas Day with our family and our new, extended family.

It gave us a focus where community came together, strangers became friends, individuals became a team with a shared purpose to make a difference - and it felt amazing!

There's a fine line between our guests and our helpers; it's run by broken biscuits, for broken biscuits, but there's an overwhelming tide of togetherness and belonging which is sometimes rare in real families.

We all believed in what we were doing. People everywhere pushed themselves to the limits to give strangers a Christmas to treasure. A whole community, working as one. A common sense of pride. A talking point but, even more so, an acting point.

Helpers who had lost people, who were alone or who just wanted a welcome distraction.

Not only has this impacted on Christmas but on other times too, with new friendships and a greater awareness, a willingness to say "Hello!" or to give an eye to those around us..

Not only have we survived Christmas, but we now get more excited about it from early November, like a child getting their hands on Argos' "laminated book of dreams" (Bill Bailey) Then it takes until the New Year to come down from it... It's difficult to describe unless you are in it.

Because no one should have no one.

To all of my friends with an empty place setting at their table today, friends who are members of a club we wish we weren't members of… have the Christmas that person would LOVE you to have.

That's the best present of all! We have learnt first hand that it is better to give than to receive. That presence is worth more than presents.

I wrote a poem - loosely in the style of the genius John Cooper Clarke - called "O Little Town of Anywhere" and recorded a Christmas 'uncommercial' with our team of helpers on a budget of £0, to inspire other communities to follow suit.

"Tis the season to be jolly…
But instead four walls,
Nobody calls.
Queen's speech, and at best, Doctor Who.
Christmas alone.
No missed calls on your phone.
It's hard to pull crackers, just you.

Love people,
Use things,
Forget all the bling.
"Just what I wanted!"
"Have you got the receipt?"

It's not Morecambe and Wise,
Twenty-seven mince pies,
Or gorging on Quality Street.

It's not all play stations,
Unwelcome relations,
Obligation as they knock at your door.

We need makers and bakers,
Cakers, movers and shakers…
Little helpers create so much more.

Children, shopping online.
Parents busy… no time!
That wasn't my "Dear Santa" letter!

Let's all give, NOT receive.
All muck in Christmas Eve,
So our Christmas can be so much better.

I don't need more socks,
Or an orange in a box,
Or yet another Toblerone.

Let's do Christmas Day,
With what we'd just throw away,
For some people who live on their own.

O little town of Anywhere,
You can do this too.
You don't need a manger, just a roomful of strangers,
Who'll all become friends, 'cos of you!

It's a simple idea, getting those who live near
And give them a day to remember,
So Christmas is Christmas, like you felt as a child,
And not just some day in December.

So - do they know it's Christmas,
If no-one comes to say
"Join us for Xmas Presence, together, Christmas Day"?

Over the past two Christmases, we have touched hundreds of people's lives. We have fed the city's homeless community, delivered gifts and meals-on-wheels to people receiving domiciliary care in the region, taken hampers of gifts to the elderly in hospital and thrown the finest Christmas party to rival any - all with a zero budget. We've given some people their first Christmas for seventeen years and had the honour of hearing some of our guests' laughter on their last ever Christmas Day. Last year, we gave one lady her final Christmas, aged 103. When her carer found her, a photo of her with us on Christmas Day had been lovingly framed and enjoyed pride of place on her mantelpiece. We were truly honoured and, yet again, a speck of dust may have got in some of our eyes. (This appears to happen a lot in this book!)

Is Xmas Presence a distraction? Yes.

Does it show us the power of community, togetherness and belonging? Yes.

Does everybody involved benefit? Yes.

Does anybody miss out? No.

Is it something to make our absent friends proud of us? Probably.

We all leave with hearts full to the brim, not only avoiding sadness but creating happiness, doing something to be immensely proud of. Where once people wanted to get up late and go to bed early to avoid Christmas, people are now getting ready early, wearing their Sunday best outfits and doing their hair. No longer a meal for one and a ping from the microwave. We are together recreating the joy of Christmases past.

Our team play Santa, hide presents, drink sherry and eat too many mince pies. Angels who haven't cracked flying yet... the values their absent parents gave them so apparent to everyone involved.

As Tiny Tim says at the end of A Christmas Carol: "God bless us, every one!"

Christmas is for children - but surely, we are ALL children, with different dates of birth...

Only Sixteen

It seems such a long time since I last saw you. I do wish we had more photos and videos of you, but you were always the one with the camera! I've pored over the computer trying to find videos to see you and hear your voice. I still think I see you sometimes - a mannerism - a posture - a walk. There are songs that come on the radio that make me think of you and remind me of you singing along, loudly, usually with the wrong words! There are still some places I can't quite face going without you too. As we became Christians together, I'm confident that you're with God in heaven and my faith continues to help get me through, but I still don't understand why though...

It's tough on my own. I don't like being a widow and I really don't like having to do all the cooking! However, I don't miss picking up your dirty socks, your moods or your snoring, but I do miss your strength, sense of humour and your talent for all things practical. Most of all I miss your big hugs.

So many people miss you. I'm not sure you ever realised how highly thought of you were. There are things I wish I could ask you too. Questions that remain unanswered...

There were times when you could be so infuriating and frustrating, but you were my husband and I loved you.

I feel so blessed to have our son.

He misses you so much. He continues to grow into such a lovely boy. You would be so very proud of him. I'm really thankful for that last family holiday we had as it gave us the opportunity to make such lovely memories together.

Keeping busy is good, but I don't ignore the grief. I can't always be strong so sometimes I allow myself to think, remember, be sad, cry and feel the pain. It's not easy and I've realised there are no shortcuts in grief. If I try to ignore it, it eventually creeps up and bites me on the bum!

So, we're doing ok. My cooking is improving (small steps), as are my (very basic) DIY skills! I am fortunate to have some truly amazing friends and family and I'm trying to look forward and discover a 'new normal', but never forgetting what we had.

It's now 20 years since, at the tender age of 22, I married you, my very tall, 36 year old Yorkshireman and this is the fourth year I've spent my wedding anniversary alone since you died. It is an odd feeling to have a date that has been so special for the two of us for so many

years and to now spend it on my own. So how do I or should I even mark it now that you've gone? The vows we exchanged said 'Til death do us part', so should I stop counting?

On the one hand I want to remember the happy day we celebrated with friends and family, the pretty dress and dodging the rain, but on the other hand it is hard to look back on those happy times alone. So what to do? Ignore it? Mark it in some way? Stay in bed, pull the curtains and shut the world out sobbing under the duvet? All completely valid options I reckon. Well, for me, the first year I just wanted to be busy allowing no time to think. I went away to visit family and we had a packed day visiting the James Bond exhibition in London (which you would've completely approved of! (Ah Mr Cole I've been expecting you.) The second year I wasn't well so

couldn't do anything much. Last year I was calming our son for day two of his SATs, scouring the internet to find the difference between a passive and an active sentence! Every year has been different, but I always bring you flowers.

Don't get me wrong, you weren't overly romantic when it came to our anniversary were you? It's not like I'm missing candlelit dinners and surprise trips to Venice, but you always got me a card and flowers (and maybe croissants for breakfast) and we'd always reminisce about how you were forced to tie your waistcoat up with butcher's string from the hotel kitchen, how a bridesmaid stood on the train of my dress as we were leaving the church and I thought it had ripped right off and how all the guests from the South wondered why on earth guests were eating cheese with apple pie at the reception, but it's just not the same reminiscing on my own.

This year I didn't have any plans. I bought my own yellow roses and brought you some too. I looked at the wedding photos and marvelled at how young we look... how our young bridesmaids are all grown up now (some with families of their own) and as the traditional gift for a 20th wedding anniversary is china, I treated myself to a new vase for the flowers.

So I will still keep counting, keep remembering, keep marking the day, but it will be forever sixteen...

Father and Son

Dear Daddy

I really miss you. It's hard not having a Dad.

I miss your cooking (I'm not saying Mummy's cooking is bad though). I wish we could still go swimming with each other together. I have started a lot of clubs like cubs, drama and football skills (but not in a team yet). I miss our father and son times at the driving range. I still remember our trip to Skye and how much fun we had. Last Christmas I got a Chelsea top in memory of your favourite football team. I have had my first two school residential trips. One to the Yorkshire Dales and one to Robin Wood. You would of loved it-there were lots of activities like a zip wire, a climbing wall and loads more. Thank you for giving me your good sense of humour and your Nerf gun!

Not many things have changed in the house. You missed the garden getting redone and I remember you were looking forward to it (it looks very nice) and it's great for playing football.

I have recently played in a tag rugby tournament and we made it through to the final . I know how much you liked rugby (by the way England didn't do very well in the Rugby World Cup. Oh well!!). I'm looking after your phone (well sort of, it's fixed now!) I always sit in your green chair. To be honest I'm surprised it's lasted this long, since you broke it! I'm in year 6 now and almost at secondary school. I wish we had more photos and videos of you, but you always had the camera in your hand. I try to think about the good times, but I wish you were still here with us.

Me and Mummy are doing well but we miss you.

I hope you're proud of me.

Love from Jonny xxxxxxxxxxxxxxxxxxxxxxxxxxxxxxxxx

The Second Time Round

"It'll never last," everybody told me. We met when I was twenty; I was twenty one in the March when he asked me to marry him and just twelve weeks later, we were man and wife!

"Marry in haste, repent at leisure!" could have been a chorus in the church but thirty years and three children later we were still together. We proved them all wrong until...

It was a Thursday night. The kids had long-since flown the nest and we were busy down-sizing. Twelve

years earlier, Sandy had suffered a heart attack. I always thought those fags would be the death of him, but he wouldn't give them up. We had plans in place to go part-time and gradually retire completely. Our life was all organised and packed in labelled boxes, ready for the move. Moving house is apparently the second most stressful thing after losing a loved one, so it said on the radio, and for the first time I could remember, I called in sick. I felt terrible.

We were both exhausted so we went to bed. It's strange how you remember the smallest detail. Will Young was singing "Leave right now" on the television and I thought "I quite like that song..."

It was ten to eleven. We'd just gone to bed, then he made a strange noise - and died. I just knew. His eyes wide open.

I rang for an ambulance and a voice at the other end of the phone told me what to do. Paramedics tried to bring him back for about an hour - then I asked them to stop. If I had gone to work that night, I would have returned the following morning not knowing if he had suffered or not. At least now I knew that he hadn't.

I can still listen to "Leave right now". I feel sad, but I don't cry over it.

I'd been away to Rome for my fiftieth birthday and gone to three weddings! I remember joking "Let's hope it's not going to be three weddings and a funeral!"

Things like this happened to old women; I always thought I would be ready for it to happen. I was about to become harder and stronger, but I had many hurdles to overcome before that transformation.

The house move had already been completed. I had no choice; I was moving from our family home, alone. I'd have given anything not to leave. If only these deals came with a 'try before you buy' offer, a '28-day sale or return' clause, I'd have pulled out in a heartbeat.

I entered a world of chaos that I can't really remember much about. Somebody stole a year of my life. It disappeared - and I disappeared with it.

We had to send three separate people to get to the kids so that no-one would hear via text massage or phone call. It was like a military operation. Just a week before, we had seen our youngest graduate to become a teacher. We were so proud!

My friend wouldn't leave me on my own - unsure if I would do something reckless - but even in the midst of this manic desperation, I knew the kids needed me. Some of my friends from way back in the '70s fed us. It meant everything because I don't think I'd even have noticed that I hadn't eaten. One even stuck a list to the fridge of what everyone drank and how they took their tea and coffee - a brilliant idea that just stopped the same question being asked again and again...

The kids were devastated, holding me, pleading with me to help them, wanting me to tell them that everything would be alright - but I couldn't. I remember making a terrible admission to them; it was simply: "I can't help you." No mother wants to utter those words, ever. But it was true.

I was broken. I couldn't fix them. I couldn't fix myself. I was in a place that none of my friends understood, nor could they reach me. I was separate, isolated from the world to which I once belonged..

My own Mum and Dad struggled with this powerless feeling. They would always try protect us from everything, but they couldn't help here.

The next day was my grandson's third birthday. He was overjoyed and excited. We sang "Happy Birthday", fighting back the tears. It wasn't his fault. We set up the back stairs as a sanctuary, somewhere for us to go, where we could take turns at crying on the bottom step.

The kids didn't cope well. I wasn't much use. The reservoir of answers, wisdom and good advice had dried up for now. I couldn't even answer my own questions.

Gradually, our dining table became a Mecca where visitors would come and sit, not to console me or to feel sorry for me, but to share happy stories and laugh with me, celebrating the man we no longer had, but who could live on through these hilarious tales.

Three doors down, we had some wonderful neighbours, Heather and Steve. They offered us so much more than a place to borrow a cup of sugar, or a helping hand to look after the guinea pigs. They would come round on a Saturday, they were always invited to family parties and my kids baby-sat for theirs. As with us, their home was to be rocked to its foundations… Cancer came for Heather when she was just forty; she left two young children. They adored their Mum. Heather had her last Christmas with the children, knowing she would soon be leaving Steve. I remember she looked at us both, to check if we would be alright, realising we were going to be in a similar situation

"We'll be fine."

I lost my husband in the November, in a split second. Steve lost his wife over time, grieving in instalments as she faded, finally losing her battle in the January.

I still hated going anywhere; there was no escape from couples! Even my own kids were coupled up. I was the remainder, the plus one, the awkward "Where can we sit her?" It was so much easier to stay in. I returned to work three months later and went out for a social drink with my manager; he was a good laugh and just let me escape over a beer.

Steve and I had things in common. Some things we wished we hadn't. We spent time together purely because nobody else got it, and we enjoyed each other's company. Then we realised this could be a 'thing'… We decided to take a week's holiday, to see if it would work.

My kids hated the idea. They thought it was too soon, but they never saw the lonely nights where I sat alone in the dark. Steve's eldest daughter was pleased for us and for herself - it meant I would share the responsibility of looking after her Dad!

Now, years down the line, somehow we are one family. I remember times when I would tell Steve to walk away from this chaos. He didn't. I never thought we'd get here, but neither of us had ever done anything wrong. Surely we all deserve to be happy?

As I said to the kids "Your Dad left me, I never left him!" Strong, hard words, but I meant them.

My kids were my life, but they were happy to see me sit in a chair, knitting. Was this to feel like some odd four-in-a-bed, where we never left our loved ones? It's like a former life almost didn't happen. Memories fade - even the good ones. This is our life now. I can edit certain bits from the past, to give it a softer focus, but I hate him for leaving me. A warning shot fired twelve years previously should have binned the cigarettes forever - but he carried on.

I remember thinking I would never find a man who would love me like he did. Now I have. I am a lucky lady. Lots of people don't even get one bite at happiness. I've had two.

My only regret is that we were too old to have a child together. That would have been perfect, but there is so much more we share together.

We have two photos of our previous partners. Their influence is still here, but we don't seem to discuss memorable anniversaries; if anything, we talk more about other people we have lost. We tend not to revisit places we went in our 'past lives'.

We are together because we want to be - not because we're young, or daft, or been going out for years and protocol suggests that we should get married. We got married for us. Full stop. We have no financial worries and only ever argue about the kids (as most couples do).

I'm back to being Mum again. The brittle, fragile shell of "me" that I became luckily didn't replace me for long. We're now introduced as parents and the kids call him Steve. One day, my daughter asked:

"Can the baby call you 'Grandad'?"

"Yes!" came the jubilant reply.

I desperately didn't want to live with Steve's children and be called 'Auntie Chris', just like a wicked Disney step-mother!

Now we live for today, because tomorrow may not be a given. We travel the world and enjoy doing what we want to do. Steve summed it all up perfectly in the opening line of his wedding speech:

"Well, who'd have thought it? Chris and me?"

Perhaps two other people who sadly couldn't be there inkling…

Could It Be Magic?

Once upon a time a man's voice appeared in a strange thing called a telephone. He couldn't fit in it but it was definitely his voice. What was this witchcraft? The day before it would have been deemed magic but on that day, it became science.

Magic is merely unproven Science. Science is proven magic. There is still so much we don't fully understand. If science was a man he'd still be in nappies. There are incidents in life that defy all probability.

Following the death of her brother Chris, Sue took a sabbatical from work returning to a new job a year later. She shared the small office with three other solicitors.

"Sue, these three will take care of you. Anything you need just ask. They'll keep you right." Said the Managing Director.

"Good morning I'm Sue."

"I'm Chris." Said the first colleague (fair enough).

"I'm Sue."

"I'm Chris." (really? Two out of two)

And finally...

"I'm Sue."

"I'm Chris." (Three out of three? A full house of new big brothers to watch over me with the same name?)

All three colleagues shared the same name as her late brother. Working on there being 40 popular girls' names, 40 popular boys' names the chances of all three colleagues being called Chris is one in 512,000 - a tiny probability or somebody sending a message that they are still keeping an eye on their little sister? Could it be magic?

There are many who believe that when you're gone you're gone - that is it -no after life, no angel on your shoulder and no ghosts.

We don't really know. So go with what works for you and what helps. Who is to say you are wrong?

Perhaps like desperate naïve audience members at an end of a pier clairvoyant show we go fishing hoping to get a bite as the back-combed charlatan says "I'm getting a J..."

(who would ever say "My name begins with a J - they'd just tell her I'm John!")

"Beginning with a J? My brother was George..."

"That's close enough" as the charlatan collects yet more hairspray vouchers from the desperate congregation.

Or like people reading yesterday's horoscopes desperately trying to hang their lives onto the hooks under Libra or Sagittarius.

For a concert at the City Varieties I had no voice at all - couldn't speak at all for two weeks previous or a week afterwards - existing on a diet of Manuka honey - I couldn't even introduce the songs. The cupboard was bare.

We had learnt all songs nearly an octave lower so Leonard Cohen or Johnny Cash could have joined in. At the sound-check my guitarist Phil said "You do realise if I play all of those songs in different keys I'll mess up every song... you'll be fine I'm sure. When the fridge door opens and the light comes on you'll be fine... you always have been"

This was different. I had no voice at all. Then something astonishing happened. I couldn't speak but for an hour I could sing. I don't know what happened nor does anyone who attended but I am eternally grateful to whoever helped that night.

In a restaurant in Manhattan four songs came on back to back from Em's Nana's funeral three days previous. Perhaps we're just tuned into them... a heightened awareness of our greatest hits as other music fades to mere ambience. I don't think so in this case as the probability of these four discreet events happening one after another would make winning the Euromillions lottery seem like rolling a dice. I refuse to believe this was a fluke.

David, a talented craftsman, orphaned aged 10, had a gypsy come up to him shouting at him in the street as an adult, saying his mother was there next to him keeping an eye on him - this could have been purely generic mumbo-jumbo but she then went on to describe her in minute detail. A wild-eyed woman too full of gin or something else?

A lady I grew up with swears that one night her late husband asked her to budge up... he was freezing. She was a down to earth woman who never exaggerated and was teetotal. She acknowledged how it sounded "far fetched" but it was real... she may be right... she may be wrong... but she was certain... and it made her happy.

Could it be magic? Perhaps it's a message to say someone is keeping an eye on us but these happen when I need them - on important days. Are we really alone?

The number 31 follows me around like a friendly shadow, houses I've lived in, classrooms I've had as form rooms, hotel rooms, tables in restaurants, hospital wards. 31 is everywhere. Perhaps I want this number to appear but even if I did I couldn't influence its prevalence in my life.

Could it be magic?

Kinloch Pride or to give its full name 'Kinloch Pride Also Ran' isn't a household name to horseracing enthusiasts. She was a wishful purchase. On the evening of her owner's funeral the television screens showed an evening race where this stranger to rosettes romped home. Why?

I was working in Berwick-upon-Tweed. Forty years previously I was stung outside the sweet shop by a bee as an 8 year old so I returned to buy my dad a tin of his favourite black bullets for Father's Day. Childhood memories came flooding back. At the counter I looked up at a scant display of brightly coloured key rings with names on them. Next to one another, as most had sold out, were Charlie and Alice on an empty stand - my Mam and Dad. Not the most common names.. surely just another coincidence or someone endorsing my purchase of his favourite childhood sweets.

On another occasion I was four miles away from Scarborough - my family's annual pilgrimage. Something strange happened like a time machine. I felt young, carefree, joyous. I passed the place where we used to play cricket, the place where we used to buy our morning paper where Jimmy Savile used to jog past...

Absent friends felt present as familiar footsteps retraced my smiles.

It felt real. It felt amazing.

I brought Dad. Having not gone there for a decade his face lit up, eyes glassy and a warm glow.

"I never thought I'd ever see this place again." He smiled.

Where he once danced down the beach, bowling and batting he was now being pushed in a wheelchair incandescently happy recalling stories at every attraction commenting what was the same and what was new.

Then as we went to go home, we turned the car to face the sea front to see the biggest rainbow frame South Bay and the harbour. It was as if it had left us a thank you for the 350 mile round journey our two day adventure took us.

We all smiled knowing what every other passenger in the car was thinking. It could just be a coincidence. It had been raining and the sun was breaking through.

Could it be magic? I hope so.

Unforgettable

This is the last page I have written for the book. I asked so much of all contributors and interviewees, yet I left mine until the eleventh hour, almost afraid to put pen to paper.

Nothing has changed me more. Marriage and parenthood were enjoyable metamorphoses, without any adverse side effects; they brought joyous change.

Losing the person who always put me first was tough, to say the least. You only get one mother. Priceless. Irreplaceable. Without her, I still wouldn't be able to tie my shoelaces! She was the cement between Dad's and my crumbly bricks. She couldn't have loved us more. It hurts as I write this that I've forgotten so much - perhaps I am only left with edited highlights. Will time trim this edit even further? I hope the half-life of remembering her means I can keep her close forever.

Worrying about this one day, I asked my Dad, sixty years after he had lost his father, "Can you still hear your Dad's voice, after all these years?"

"No."

Then he walked tentatively for five more steps…

"Yes, I can! I CAN still hear him!"

Dad went from hurt to happiness in a few feet. This is my greatest fear; I don't want to forget.

To the untrained on-looker, we appeared very different, but we were similar in so many ways. We could lock horns like stags; we were cut from similar cloth - both worriers, loyal, caring and loving - with everyone entitled to our opinions.

Mam gave our Annie and me her eyes that now gaze back from the mirror. Why is it that we stare more closely when we're feeling terrible? I often think "If I live to be as old as you, I have fifteen years left." That can't happen! Mam's also cost me a fortune in "Just for Badgers", thanks to our genes which meant we went grey in our early twenties.

As I write this, Little Ted, the bear I was given the day I was born, sits on top of my wardrobe. I have lived in over twenty houses since leaving Tow Law in 1988 and have no idea how Ted got there! But he's there somehow… Could it be magic?

Whenever I see biscuits, cake or crisps I still smile. Mam claimed to never like any of them, yet I can't remember a day without them passing her lips, even if she was "slimming" - she never, ever referred to it as "dieting"!

"It was in the sale!" she'd announce proudly as she came through the

door laden with 'essentials'. "You'll not believe how much I saved today!"

She could spend! Dad never had a clue, but it didn't seem to matter as he always had money to buy a new car every two years, so all must have been OK.Mam was an expert personal shopper, long before the term existed.She could hold up any garment and know if it would fit either me or my Dad's well-furnished frames in an instant. I had more Adidas tee-shirts than the factory in Germany! She always insisted on paying and would react aggressively if we ever tried to treat her for a change.

She loved Christmas and would cover our house in every non-fire-resistant decoration Woolworth's had! There are still remnants of Sellotape and festive debris on Dad's ceiling to this day, I'm sure. Woolies' demise coincided with Mam no longer being here to buy their pick'n'mix and Christmas decs!

Not quite a hypochondriac, but she loved a good ailment and would often share any new prescription she'd been given. I've inherited this; I'm resilient, never miss work, but still whinge about the slightest niggle…

I'm so glad she missed Cilla and Wogan dying; she'd have been in bits! I remember snuggling up for Children in Need, blubbing in stereo to Surprise Surprise and Challenge Anneka. Mam always out-scored Bill Beaumont and Emlyn Hughes on A

Question of Sport and never failed to identify the mystery sportsman.

I didn't always make her proud though... "I've raised a heathen!" - this because I never became a good Methodist and expelled myself from Sunday School!

She loved football, but refused to watch Match of the Day whenever Newcastle had lost, resulting in many an early Saturday night. Despite being happily married for forty years, Mam always had eyes for another man...

"Trevor Brooking! What a gentleman he is, with lovely thick curly hair... AND he was a good scholar; he's got excellent A-levels!" I always felt my Dad was on borrowed time if West Ham's former favourite ever came knocking.

Perfect Yorkshire puddings and Oxo in everything. She boiled vegetables as if they had committed a medieval atrocity- and insisted my dad didn't eat spicy food.

Dad was the love of her life. She didn't have to walk the full length of the counter; Dad picked her from the tree, not the barrel... from keeping score for his basketball team, to a first date with The Who, to turning down his wedding proposal unless he stopped his 60-a day Senior Service habit - he was a 1960s' PE teacher after all! They all smoked like chimneys!

Not having my Mam hurts more than I can say-but it hurts so much more

to see Dad without her. In many ways, couples should go together... I often wonder, if that was offered as an option - as an extra wedding vow - how many would take it up? What would be the impact on society if they did? For better or for worse?

One thing is certain - it was Mam who made me love music, which changed my life forever and is now changing my children's lives. Her records formed the soundtrack of my growing up. Her radiogram was a treasure chest of 3-minute wonders that are still in my Top Ten. As I write this, a playlist of John Lennon, Crystal Gayle, The Carpenters, Dolly Parton and Chicago makes the ink run out so much quicker and adds a glassy appearance to the page, but these old friends still feel magical.

After every training course I do, I play "Sam" by Olivia Newton-John - and smile. There's no such thing as a guilty pleasure; there's merely pleasure, and those songs make me happy and sad in equal measure. I can hear Mam singing along in every bar of those songs as if she's still drying the pots in the kitchen.

Whenever I've needed a sign or a helping hand, a song appears from nowhere. It happens far too often for it to be a fluke. Up until 2009, I always felt as if I was swimming against the tide. Since Mam died, it's changed completely. Whenever I need a green light, I get one. I regularly meet people who come from nowhere when I need them. Perhaps we make our own luck, and reap what we sow, but I still think there's something else and I like that idea. It reminds of a line from "This" by Darius Rucker:

"I cried when my Mama passed away,

But now I've got an angel looking out for me today,

So nothing's a mistake."

Mam loved doing things for others. She brought the best out in children and older people. I've tried to follow suit. She would adore everything I'm doing now...

I loved seeing her face light up as I played shows at The Grand Opera House, only to be met after the show with "those shoes haven't seen a polish!" - just in case I ever got ideas above my station from the standing ovations.

I was once asked "if you could have a dinner party and invite anybody from history, who would you invite?"

I would ignore the usual suspects like Marilyn Monroe, Muhammad Ali, Jesus and Einstein. I would have my kids, my Dad, my Mam and my sister - who was short-changed, having seventeen years less of Mam than I had - and the two grandchildren Mam never met. Keep your icons - they're merely posters on a bedroom wall, pub quiz answers, apparently significant figures of the 20th century, but my history is far more local. I don't think Muhammad Ali would get a word in anyhow, as my

Mam would have too much to catch up on!

She gave me a change of career from out of the blue. I have matched her unwavering self-discipline with cake, biscuits and crisps!

"If I could put another smile on your face,

If I could put another beat within your heart,

Put another breath on your lips -

I'd kiss it better."

I wrote these words in a song to help me through tough times. Eight years on, 31 Campbell Street is still Mam's house. It still smells of her... it's still full of her. Nothing has changed; she just lets Dad live in it.

It was so hard to watch someone who gave me my first breaths suffocating in a room full of air. We take breathing as a given; I saw it become a luxury. To see a machine attempt to replicate what our lungs do without thinking shows what a gift life truly is.

She died at 62. We never knew how ill she was. For years, she had said she had every ailment going but, when the big one came, she kept it to herself. Selfish? Unselfish? Her decision. There was no chance for the kids to say goodbye. We had no run up before the call came that Friday night at 9:10pm.

I'm so thankful that I felt an odd urgency to bring her and Dad down to us for Father's Day. It was a stunning day - the sun shone and we had so much fun and good eating in the garden. We never do that!

That was our last day together

She'd be amazed that Dad has learnt to recreate her greatest hits - but has never mastered ironing! He refuses to tolerate Emmerdale and the only other woman in his life has been Rachel Riley, ever since Carol Vorderman also "left" him. Nowadays Dad and I can swear out loud... losing Mam was a high price just to swear in front of one another.

I remember having to play a gig on July 4th - the day I was told she had less than forty eight hours to live. I couldn't not do it. She'd have been appalled if I'd let someone down, so I went to the gig, to the astonishment of the lads in the band. I told the high maintenance promoter to keep out of my face, for fear of being eaten alive by my raw emotion. I then went on, to hide in clear view of five hundred people for two hours. The spotlight is a strangely warm and soothing haven to escape reality. As Humphrey Lyttleton once said, "Doctor Gig will heal all."

It didn't, but it got me through. I picked up the phone to talk to Dad at 2am.

"See you tomorrow, lad."

Two days later, Mam died, unable to breathe without the aid of a feat of engineering. I never take breathing for granted. Lung cancer took a staunch non-smoker. In that one moment, I lost my biggest supporter, my proudest fan and, on her day, my biggest adversary, but one thing was never questioned... She always loved me.

I have learnt more in the eight years without her than I learnt in the previous thirty nine. Our relationship seems stronger without words; I know so much more. I've learnt what matters, who matters and what doesn't. I think Mam would love everything I'm doing now and everything I stand for. She inspired me to write this book.

Mam taught me everything, except how to live without her.

On The Beach

I miss not being able to hear the little chuckles when we are watching a programme, knowing we both 'got' the joke-when it passed others by.Thank you for giving me the opportunity to share your journey, even if your ticket only took you part of the way to stop number 49. I still feel guilty if I pass any of your photos and don't stop to blow a kiss or say something to you.

The only thing certain in life is death. You just got your ticket off this planet before I did. Someone has to stick around to sort out the paperwork after all...

I wish someone had said to me

"Before you throw out those items, or fill the charity shop , take photos take samples and make notes and take more time to think about whether you are ready yet to let go of them yet because when they're gone they're gone!"

Our photos of happy holidays comfort me but I'm also glad I took photos and videos of the times you were poorly towards the end. These darker images of the torment of Huntington's Disease help me make sense of your death being a release and a positive thing for you in that respect.

Thank you to those who understand that even after several years I am content pottering along and getting on with my own grief. I wish those who seem to think I should take steps to 'move on' would keep their good intentions to themselves.

Time helps to erode the sharpness of the pain of grief. Initially it's like walking on a beach of sharp shards of glass barefoot. As time goes on, the tide of tears and time washes over the glass strewn beach. It smooths out the sharpness making it feel more like walking on pebbles. Still a bit painful underfoot but bearable. The burning sun of memories can sometimes make the pebbles too hot and make you want to step off quickly or the powerful waves of emotion can make you too scared that you will get knocked off your feet.

With time the pebbles change to walking on a calm and sandy beach. The sensation underfoot becomes more comfortable. The beach is more a place where you want to visit to relax to watch the grains of grief gently running through your fingers; mixed with tears to build sandcastles of memories.

The sun on your face; the castles in the sun; and the lap of gentle waves of emotion bringing a kind of inner peace. Everyone knows, there's nothing more lovely than sitting in a peaceful place and looking up to the sky towards what could be a form of Heaven, whatever that is, wondering who is up there sharing the moment and smiling back at you.

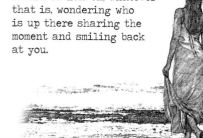

All You Need Is Love...

The good news is that if you have got this far in the book, you've maintained your 100% survival record mentioned earlier. Congratulations!

Whether this has been read from coffee table, iPad, Kindle, lying in bed or sitting on the toilet, I hope it has helped in some way. You've peered behind many a curtain as brave contributors have shared their stories, with varying outcomes. They may have found a route so far through their grief but, unfortunately, their footprints probably won't work for you. It's like finding the text book with pencil notes from the cleverest student in the year above; you still have to put in the effort and work at it. Sadly, we can't crib their answers; copy and paste is rarely a true solution. If only it was that simple. You may have realised, too late, how wonderful your life was before.

"Regrets? I've had a few, but then again, too few to mention.

More, much more than this, you'll do it YOUR way..."

I hope that you have gleaned from these stories that grieving isn't a fast process... you have to go at its pace. Take as much time as you need - but you can do this. You may never get over it, you may simply get through it - but keep going. We are all 'Work in Progress'. We are all 'Men at Work'.

Hopefully you've caught some of the ideas thrown up in the air here to help, or at least to spark a conversation. I also hope that reading these chapters has shown you that you're not the only one; it's not just you after all! We're all a bit of a mess. In many cases, the only person who doubts your abilities may be YOU! Despite what Forrest Gump said, the world isn't a box of chocolates; it's more like a tin of broken biscuits. We can either dwell on the cracks or make the best cheesecake ever!

Think about the person you have lost. What have they given you? What traits and values from them lie deep within you? What can you do today to make them happy and proud? To be the best "you" they'd love to see? You DESERVE to be happy.

Following the death of a loved one, our priorities may change from seeking money, success and material

Image by Yellow Mustang Photography

the wrong ones, but times, situations and people can all change. Some of the best friends you make later in life, 'fit' better; we don't wear the same clothes we did when we were twenty. I'm not saying friends are disposable, but some dispose of themselves through their actions and inactions. As we grow older, perhaps we tolerate some people less as we become aware of how finite time is.

Grieving is like playing a musical instrument or a sport - you're never finished, you just get better, but occasionally there's a day when your fingers are all over the place. Even the most skilful golfers get stuck in a bunker. We all have differently shaped holes in our futures. We shouldn't try to hammer a "you"-shaped peg into a square hole; we need to create that "you"-shaped hole - and that's going to take time, effort, understanding and care.

We strive to create. We don't want to simply "cope"; we deserve to live. We want to have reasons to jump out of bed on a morning, to enjoy the gift of life, to thrive, not survive - and in time, we want to appreciate our new "normal". It's clear that hurt is widespread, though not necessarily fairly spread, across the world. Paddy McAloon wrote "once more the sound of crying is no.1 across the Earth". That has been - and will always be - the case.

Wouldn't it be great if life was the perfect length, like your favourite film, where it was eventful and

things to finding happiness, remembering to use things and love people, to making the most of our precious time. Killing time is both crime and punishment rolled into one, when you look back on a wasted life. The relationship that changes is the one with yourself, because that's the only person who can really help you. The best friend you may ever find may be looking back at you from the mirror.

"Learning to love yourself is the greatest love of all" - Linda Creed.

If you can be happy with that person alone, finding your own company is good company - and everybody else is a bonus! Choose your friends carefully. Don't keep them simply because you've had them a long time; you might need a clearout once in a while; you might need to shuffle your pack. It's an odd feeling, as if you have chosen happy, with the odd drama along the way? "Thanks, you've been great... touched so many lives... made a few mistakes, but overall, your life has been something to be proud of. Come on, you must be tired. Sleep well."

You can't play God with your own life, but you can try to improve someone else's, making a difference wherever possible, not sticking but twisting, still taking risks. A life without risk is a mere existence.

Tomorrow isn't a given. Tomorrow may not happen. That's why TODAY is the most important day of your life! Don't let regret darken your day. Forgive yourself for past indiscretions - the things you said or didn't say, the things you did or didn't do. Saving up for rainy days is all about being careful. Why not be reckless? We're obsessed with Yesterday and Tomorrow, often forgetting about Today. Don't save bucket-lists for dying; tick the items off when you're full of life. You can't fatten up a calf on market day. Life is all about the relationships we share together. Solitary confinement - extreme loneliness - is deemed the toughest of all punishments.

"It's the loneliness that's the killer"- Seal.

The sooner we all call an amnesty on the truth, the better. Every pub, restaurant, workplace or school has people carrying on after losing loved ones. We're all bluffing our way through tough situations...

nobody is "the man"! Nobody is "normal", because nobody was asked what NORMAL was! It's an imaginary origin on a pair of axes we think we are miles away from. It's as if we're all at the same party, in ill-fitting clothes, squeezing ourselves into Spanx that are torturing us underneath. We all feel incredibly uncomfortable while we try to fool one another that we're in better shape than we really are. The joke is, we're ALL wearing them, so why don't we come clean, remove these elasticated shackles and relax with one another in comfort? The world isn't photo-shopped or airbrushed - let's just be us. If you surround yourself with the right people, they'll thank you for it.

So, next time you're thinking of having a go at someone in a shop, stop and ask yourself "what are they going through today? What invisible baggage are they carrying, that they had no choice in packing?" How would you like to be spoken to, if you were them? Is your "3 out of 10" that you're raising your voice for, really a 3? Is it honestly as big a deal as you think? If not, then cut them the slack you would like to have cut for you, if you were in their position. Somebody else might well consider your 3/10 a 9! As my friend Pricey may have said "DIM:DIF!"

In writing this book, it's become clear that small acts of kindness will be remembered forever. Mark Twain knew that "kindness is the language that the blind can see and the deaf can hear" so in future, if you are ever in doubt about how you should behave, always be KIND. If you can help, HELP!

Despite what the media might suggest, the world is not broken. Newspapers may tell us that the manufacturing industry has died in this country, but we can manufacture the most important product of all at no cost... happiness. If we help others, it makes them happy - and us! Why don't we do this more? It's a win win! Nobody loses. There are so many amazing, inspirational people around you who are willing to avoid the over-crowded path of least resistance and will go the extra mile to help you, when you need it most.

This book has made me look at resilience in a different way. Psychologists describe resilience as "the capacity to recover quickly from difficulties" and JK Rowling says that "Strength comes from adversity". I always thought resilience was tough and hard, like a suit of armour. Meeting all these people while writing this has shown me that resilience is soft, gentle, optimistic, warm and caring. People love more, not less and they allow people in rather than block them out. Resilience is strong - and it's one of the most beautiful qualities in life.

If you have lost someone, always remember:

If you can still see them,

If you can still hear them,

If you can still smell them,

If you can remember their touch and the way they made you feel...

...have you really lost them? Or just some part of them? Have we lost the box, but the chocolates remain all around us, within us and our children? What 'foolish things' can you use, to help you remember them, and smile? How are you keeping them alive, or close to you, every day? (And by the way, if you've put a brass plaque on a park bench for someone you love, I'm sure its lovely!).

Enjoy people today. Don't tap on your phone, impressing people who don't matter! One day, you may look back on the pie chart of how much time you've spent seeking the validation of insignificant others, whilst the significant ones who matter, die.

Lennon and McCartney told us "All you need is love" but love is to be shared together, today, when we're alive, because it can't be left in a will. Too many people live life as if they're going to get another draft. Remember as a child how desperate you were to make snowmen when the snow was melting? Learn from that. As the Specials' hit goes "Enjoy yourself, it's later than you think!"

This next metaphor may not be the most beautiful image I've used in the book, but I've a feeling it'll be shared far and wide, to sum up how precious time is...

"The toilet roll runs out much quicker the nearer you get to the cardboard."

Time is an odd currency with fluctuating exchange rates... sometimes flying, other times dragging, but one fact remains: there is never enough time. So there is only one way to do this... YOUR way! You have to create YOUR survival kit, to fit YOU. Share what works and share what doesn't, so mistakes should only be made once. Surround yourself with the right people who "get" you; you don't find out if a boat is any good by sailing it on a mill pond.

Relationships are everything. Don't be afraid of someone who is grieving; do all you can to help them, in words and deeds. If there's a basket of snakes, hissing in the corner, sometimes the only way for them to leave is to dare to open the lid.

Unfortunately, reaching this last page won't coincide with "Grief download completed" on your new iGrieve app - it's not that easy! - but if it's got you talking, that's a step in the right direction. After you've had a broken leg, you may limp for a while, but you'll be walking again. In time, you'll realise what you can influence and what you can't. Get to a point where what you think, say and do, all completely overlap.

Whilst writing this book, I have sought, enjoyed and valued the opinions and wisdom of children and older people. Perhaps we should all listen to these generations more? Unfortunately, the world's decision makers are in the generation in-between; they think they're the clever ones!

It seems only fitting to end the book with a pearl of wisdom from an 8-year old, my son, Billy. One day, after seeing people dying on the news, Billy said, "Dad, I've been thinking..." (Often ominous!) "If you give an eye to me and make sure I'm OK, and not doing anything silly, and you look after me, and we keep an eye on Mum, then we help Rob and Charlotte next door, and they keep an eye on us, and we make sure Hannah and Michael are alright, and we all just look after one another... isn't that the world sorted?"

"Yes."

The End.

It's All About You

After speaking to hundreds of people, here is a pick'n'mix of pearls of wisdom, things that have worked for them and helped them keep going.

See which ones fit you, and put them in your pocket for later...

- One thing is certain - everybody you meet is an expert who will know what's best for you, but only you are an expert in YOU!

- Listen to yourself - tune into "Radio YOU" and look for YOUtopia.

- Realise what you can control - and what you can't.

- Be selfish occasionally.

- Keep your lost loved one's mobile number on your phone, if it helps.

- If you block things out, it may look as if you're making progress, but it may stifle any change long term.

- Don't fake happiness to try to fool yourself. Fake happiness is so much worse than genuine sadness.

- Prepare yourself in the lead up to significant dates such as birthdays, Christmas, Father's Day, New Year etc.

- Don't beat yourself up about having useless friends. It says more about them than it does about you. Times change. Some friends are Parker pens, some are Bic biros, some are forever friends, some are just passing through...

- Avoid comparing life now to life before by trying something totally new.

- Care for others if you can - it gives you a purpose. Try not to be at the end of the care chain.

- If you need to hibernate under a duvet, just do it!

- Don't be strong for ANYONE!

- Never let your standards drop. Stay classy. Bridges weren't meant to be burnt.

- Write things down or keep a diary to see where you were, where you are and how you got there.

- Look after yourself; alcohol may look like a friend but be wary because it comes at a price. The fitter you are, the better you are able to cope, both mentally and physically. Alcohol is a friend who tells you what you want to hear but will punch you in the face the following day. You wouldn't tolerate this behaviour from any other friend.

- The more you can keep a clear head, the more mornings become your friend and you can achieve more.

- Allow others to help you. Let them in when you feel you can.

- Acknowledge people's help, no matter how little use it is; they mean well and are on your side.

- Keep score of how you are feeling and how you can influence it.

- Allow down time to be rubbish and do nothing. Inactivity can be just the activity you need that day.

- Don't just surround yourself with people - surround yourself with the RIGHT people.

- Talk and listen to those who care and for whom you care about.

- Realise that today is tomorrow's "good old days", so make them special.

- Read throwaway, trashy novels or deep, meaningful texts and get lost in words. Anything that broadens the mind, challenges you or can give you even a crumb of help can be invaluable.

- Be busy, but not too busy to think and reflect. It's hard to appreciate the painting if your nose is pressed up against it all of the time.

- Never write you off.

- Don't make decisions in haste that you may regret.

- Don't make too many changes at once.

- Don't keep doing things that make someone else happy if it doesn't make you happy.

- Don't beat yourself up with "what ifs" and "if onlys".

- Whenever you feel like you are in limbo or unable to get out of a rut, change your environment. If a plant can't grow, we change its environment to allow it to flourish.

- The more fresh air you can get, the better - cycle, dog-walking, visit the coast, open-water swimming... Prisoners are left in solitary confinement with nothing but four walls as a brutal punishment - you aren't!

- Don't be afraid of saying NO.

- Don't be afraid of saying YES.

- Keep a diary. You may surprise yourself in time with just how far you have come.

- Don't be afraid to ask for medical advice and if you need medication, take it. You wouldn't think twice if you had a physical problem...

- Don't pretend to be stronger than you are; it may fool others, but not the person whose true opinion really matters - YOURS!

- The first rule of first aid is: take care of YOU!

- Never underestimate the power of a small act of kindness; It will be remembered many years into the future.

- Listen to the radio - it's more like an intimate conversation, playing to an audience of one, rather than television that often plays to a crowd.

- Don't waste time! Make lists to give yourself things to do, a la "One Minute Manager", and use this idea to set yourself bitesize tasks which take up thirty minutes at a time - "Lists saved my life!"

- Write down precious memories and cherish what you have been given.

- Do things that make you happy, no matter how ridiculous. There is no such thing as a guilty pleasure... there is just pleasure.

- Learn new skills - guitar, piano, kick-boxing, painting, poetry...

- Do WHATEVER you need to do to be the best "you" that you can be - and the "you" that your absent friend would love to see today.

Life is about trial and error. Never be afraid to fail - that way, you will always have a better chance of succeeding.

My way...

Thank You

I have so many people to thank and I will probably have missed people... if I have please forgive me...

My Mam & Dad

Em, Annie & Billy who have put up with so much as I wrote this

Thanks to Helen Binks, Anna Donaghy, Julian Cole, Inny Hashim for tolerating by blatant disregard and indiscipline re grammar and punctuation and making it vaguely readable

Leisa Sherry for making this book look warm and beautiful!

Stuart & Rachel for believing in "The Missing Peace" from it's inception

Johnny Mcgough for being my sounding board on a daily basis

Hairdressers everywhere who are the world's unpaid counsellors! It's not all "are you going out tonight?" and "have you been on your holidays?"

Jo Cole for being my 'one man veto' for the book

Simon Wallace for being amazing at everything I am terrible at.

Amanda & Anton

Kirsty & Chub Perkins

Stuart & Jenny Wilkinson

Johnny Thirkell

Sue O'Donnell

Dilly & Barry

Karen Boyes

Bereaved Childrens Support York

Marc McGarraghy at Yellow Mustang Photography

All friends at Wellburn Care

Gordon Train

Diane Waddell-Brown

Andrew Carr

George Hall

Martin Ledger
Sarah Frank
Paul Meehan
Trish Dainton
Rachel & Steve
Olwyn
Lou Squires
Ellie Holmes
Wayne Dixson
Mark Hodgson
Davy Harrison
Pete Harrington
Alison Redhead
Guy Mowbray
Steve Davis
Little Sarah
Davina
Angela Rippon OBE
Graham Hodge
Sally Sanderson
Josh Benson
Riccall Carers
Xmas Presence team past & present
Kevin Curran
Inspired Youth
Cherie Bakewell
Charles Hutchinson at York Press
Jon Cowap at BBC Radio York
Ben & Ellie at Minster FM
BBC Look North
Team Steel
Jane Leach
Yvie Wonder

Chris Lowther
Tow Law
Alison & all at Peregrine House
Suzy's Open Heart
Doc of Ages Sophie
Chris Mitchell
Gemma Macdonald
Andy & Will at Dr. Shakamotos Studio
All NIGHT TO REMEMBER team
All FB friends & twitterati
Everybody who tolerates my chaos on
a daily basis

To everybody who is the friend to
others in their darkest hours to
walk beside them and hold their
hand.
You matter by showing others... THEY
matter.

Printed in Great Britain
by Amazon